SO YOU WANT TO BE A FILM OR TV DIRECTOR?

Amy Dunkleberger

Enslow Publishers, Inc.
40 Industrial Road
Box 398
Berkeley Heights, NJ 07922
USA

http://www.enslow.com

Library of Congress Cataloging-in-Publication Data

Dunkleberger, Amy.
    So you want to be a film or TV director? / by Amy Dunkleberger. — 1st ed.
        p. cm. — (Careers in film and television)
    Includes bibliographical references and index.
    ISBN-13: 978-0-7660-2738-1
    ISBN-10: 0-7660-2738-4
    1. Motion pictures—Production and direction—Vocational guidance—Juvenile literature.
    2. Television—Production and direction—Vocational guidance—Juvenile literature. I. Title.
    II. Series.
    PN1995.9.P75D78 2007
    791.4302'33023—dc22

                                                    2006009733

Printed in the United States of America

10 9 8 7 6 5 4 3 2 1

To Our Readers:
We have done our best to make sure all Internet addresses in this book were active and
appropriate when we went to press. However, the author and the publisher have no control over
and assume no liability for the material available on those Internet sites or on other Web sites
they may link to. Any comments or suggestions can be sent by e-mail to
comments@enslow.com or to the address on the back cover.

Illustration Credits: All images courtesy of the Everett Collection, Inc., except p. 6,
Library of Congress; and p. 32, Jupiterimages Corporation.

Cover Illustration: Stock disc/Getty Images.

CONTENTS

INTRODUCTION

Directors. According to an old joke, everybody wants to be one, but what exactly do they do? The dictionary defines a movie director as the person who supervises the creative aspects of a film and instructs the actors and crew. Directors do not write the scripts, but they know how to visualize them; they do not photograph the action, but they know where to put the camera; they do not edit the footage, but they know what to cut. In short, directors do a little bit of just about everything.

The best directors are jack-of-all-trades, overseeing every aspect of the filmmaking process. Only the producer spends as much time on a given movie as the director. From rewriting the opening scene to tweaking the final edit, directors have influence over every step of the creative process.

In its loosest sense, the history of directing is synonymous with the history of film itself. The moment that motion pictures graduated from photographic oddity to story-telling medium, the movie director was born.

EDWIN S. PORTER

In America, the most influential early motion picture director was Edwin S. Porter. Porter, who was born in 1870, began his film career in the 1890s as an exhibitor and equipment manufacturer. In 1900, while employed at inventor Thomas Edison's movie company, Porter teamed up with actor and scenic designer George S. Fleming to produce a series of very short silent films.

These early films consisted of a single scene enacted in front of a fixed, eye-level camera. Movies like *Kansas Saloon Smashers* (1901) and *Why Mr. Nation Wants a Divorce* (1901) contained one or two shots and ran less than a minute. Porter operated the camera, then developed and put together the footage. Over the next year or so, Porter added more and more shots to his films, cutting and combining them to show dramatic action in a new, purely visual way.

In his 1903 release, *The Great Train Robbery*, Porter advanced editing methods ever further and added modest camera movement, more varied camera placement, and location shooting to his roster of filmmaking techniques. *The Great Train Robbery* also marked the debut of cinema's first western star, Broncho Billy Anderson, and established westerns as a favorite movie genre.

D. W. GRIFFITH

The next wave of movie innovation began in 1908 with the emergence of director D. W. Griffith (1875–1948). Most film scholars consider Griffith the most important figure in the development of film as an art form, and he has been called by many "the father of film language."

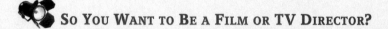

A few scenes from The Great Train Robbery, *produced and directed by Edwin Porter in 1903.*

A native of Kentucky, Griffith first worked as a stage actor and playwright, drifting into motion pictures out of financial necessity. While acting in and writing film stories for the Biograph Company, Griffith was asked to fill in for a sick director on an upcoming production, *The Adventures of Dollie* (1908). That short film became the first of over 400 that Griffith directed between 1908 and 1913.

During those five years, Griffith expanded on and enhanced editing and photographic techniques introduced by Porter. Guided by his superb cameraman, Billy Bitzer, Griffith made the camera even more fluid and used lighting for effect like never before. His intricate editing and shot selection drew audiences deeper into the world of the film.

In short movies like *The Lonedale Operator* (1911) and *A Beast at Bay* (1912), Griffith advanced the art of the action sequence. He also oversaw the emergence of a new, more subtle style of movie acting, made famous by such silent stars as Lillian Gish and Mary Pickford.

In 1915, Griffith released the film he is best known for, *The Birth of a Nation*. Because of its sympathetic portrayal of the post-Civil War Ku Klux Klan, *The Birth of a Nation* has long been a contro-versial picture, but its place in cinema history remains. At three hours, *The Birth of a Nation* became American cinema's first epic. (The 1914 Italian film, *Cabiria*, which also ran about three hours, is considered the original film epic.) With its night photography, large cast, and original musical score (played by a live orchestra), the movie's scope and artistry stunned audiences of the day.

Griffith and a select group of director-performers, including Charlie Chaplin and Buster Keaton, dominated the Hollywood movie industry for the next ten years. In Europe, German directors like F. W. Murnau and Fritz Lang introduced the world to expressionism, a type of filmmaking in which time and space are distorted.

In the late 1920s, film added another element to its art—sound. Silent movie title cards—on which brief lines of dialogue or description were printed—were replaced by spoken dialogue. Integrated music scores replaced live musical accompaniment, and movie musicals became hugely popular.

Early sound films tended to be stilted and talky, but directors like Alfred Hitchcock, Rouben Mamoulian, and Fritz Lang found new ways to blend sound and music to increase dramatic tension. Other Hollywood directors, like Ernst Lubitsch and Howard Hawks, revolutionized movie dialogue by making it fast and smart.

During the 1940s and 1950s, cinema began a gradual shift toward realism. Movie acting became more natural and the camera more fluid. Prominent Hollywood directors included John Ford, Billy Wilder, George Stevens, and Orson Welles. While still making commercial films within the studio system, these directors created movies with an identifiable style.

THE *AUTEUR* THEORY

In the early 1950s, French movie critics began using the term *auteur* to describe these distinctive film directors. According to the *auteur* theory, more than the screenwriter, producer, or star, the director is the major creative force behind any movie. In films made by *auteurs* (French for authors), the critics argued, the personality, or personal stamp, of the director is plain to see. A director's stamp might be obvious in the look of the pictures—their visual style—and/or in the subject matter or genre of the stories.

Coinciding with the *auteur* theory, European filmmakers like Federico Fellini and Francois Truffaut rose to international prominence in the late 1950s and 1960s. Their films, including Truffaut's *The 400 Blows* (1959) and Fellini's *8½* (1963), combined psychological realism with bold visual experimentation. These movies were highly personal, both in terms of their visuals and their stories, and had a tremendous influence on young filmmakers in America.

Today, directors like Quentin Tarantino (*Pulp Fiction*, *Kill Bill*) and Tim Burton (*Big Fish*, *Charlie and the Chocolate Factory*), whose artistic styles are very recognizable, are called *auteurs*. Because it tends to diminish or even dismiss the contributions of other film collaborators, however, the *auteur* theory has always been controversial.

Nevertheless, directors continue to enjoy the distinction of being the "name" behind the movie.

ELEMENTS OF DIRECTING:
FROM THE SCRIPT TO THE SHOT

No matter what type of story is being told, the starting point for every director is the movie script. From beginning to end, the screenplay supplies the impetus for most artistic decisions a director makes. It is his or her creative touchstone. Director Cameron Crowe (*Almost Famous, Elizabethtown*) described the importance of the script this way: "For me, it begins with writing, because writing is so much a part of the filmmaking process. You're always writing. You're writing on film."[1]

GENRE

How does a director translate words on a page to images on a screen? The first step in the process involves the script itself. What genre, or type, of story is it? Action-adventure? Suspense? Romantic comedy?

Like all artists, directors make choices based on their backgrounds and personalities. Some directors, like Tim Burton and Ridley Scott (*Blade Runner, Kingdom of Heaven*), have graphic arts backgrounds and approach stories very visually. Because of their early training, these directors tend to see drama more in terms of pictures than words.

Other directors, like Woody Allen (*Hannah and Her Sisters, Match Point*) and Alexander Payne (*Election, Sideways*), began their careers as writers and/or theater directors and emphasize character interaction over physical action. They are more likely

Director Tim Burton (left) chats with actor Vincent Price on the set of Edward Scissorhands *(1990).*

to direct comedies, romances, and any story with complex characters.

Regardless of background, however, a good director understands that in order to keep an audience interested, the movie must engage both the mind and the eye. A good director leaves nothing to chance. If a screenplay is well written, a part of the director's job will already be done. Dramatic situations and emotions will already be translated into concrete, filmable behaviors. The director's task then is to discover the most compelling way to bring these behaviors alive on screen.

WHAT'S IT ALL ABOUT?

Once a script has been selected, the initial question most directors ask is: what is this story about? In his book *Making Movies*, longtime director Sidney Lumet (*Twelve Angry Men, Find Me Guilty*) notes that for him "the theme (the what of the movie) is going to determine the style (the how of a movie)."[2]

The next question a director will ask is: Who is the story's main character, or protagonist? From whose perspective is the story being told? The director will then think about the film's plot and structure, and what obstacles have been included to create dramatic tension. The director will note turning points in the action and how the story reaches its climax.

After getting an overall sense of a film's story, the director will begin to look at the script in terms of visuals and performance. According to Steven Spielberg (*E.T., War of the Worlds*), "How a film should look is just trial and error and living with it for a while. I try to figure out what kind of story it's supposed to be. . . . I'm pretty prepared before I shoot a picture. I know the look, the style. I know the energy and the tone."[3]

Every story has its requirements and challenges, and every production has its restrictions. Budget restrictions can limit a director's choices but can also inspire experimentation. When breaking down a script, directors must determine how, using the tools and budget at their disposal—actors, cameras, settings, etc.—they can make the story work.

Before shooting begins, directors consult with their cinematographers and production designers. Among other concerns, cinematographers help directors make lighting and camera choices, while production designers make suggestions for settings, props, and décor. In fact, every member of the creative team, including music composers and costume designers, will at some point discuss the script with the director.

> **CINEMATOGRAPHER—**
> The technician responsible for photographing a scene and often for the overall look of a film. Also called director of photography.

> **PRODUCTION DESIGNER—**
> Person responsible for the look and feel of a film's setting and costumes.

THE SHOT

The most basic visual unit in film is the shot. A shot is defined as all images that are recorded continuously by a movie camera, from the time the camera starts to the time it stops. A shot can be as short or long as the camera's technology allows (usually between one second and half

> **FRAME—**A single image or photograph from a strip of film; or the borders encompassing the image.

Director Steven Spielberg at work on the set.

an hour). It can be as completely still, with neither camera nor objects moving, or it can be very active, with both camera and objects in motion.

Although the audience does not literally see it, as they would with a painting, shots are contained within a frame. With a few exceptions, all shots in a given movie have the same sized frame—that is, their horizontal and vertical ratios (height vs. width) remain constant throughout. The contents of a shot—what objects are placed within the frame and how they are arranged and move—is called *mise-en-scène*.

CREATING *MISE-EN-SCÈNE*

In his book *Understanding Movies*, film historian Louis Giannetti notes that *mise-en-scène* "resembles the art of painting in that an image of formal patterns and shapes is presented on a flat surface and enclosed within a frame. But because of its theatrical heritage, cinematic *mise-en-scène* is also an expression of a dramatic idea, which is determined by a context in time."[4] In other words, film *mise-en-scène* includes the passage of time that is inherent in storytelling. It encompasses both the composition of an image and any movement that occurs during the shot. *Mise-en-scène* exists in order to advance the storytelling, to take the viewer from Point A to Point B. It is the director's job to decide the *mise-en-scène* of each shot.

> *MISE-EN-SCÈNE—*
> The arrangement of objects and their movement within a shot.

SIZE

When composing a shot, the director first decides which objects—actors and/or scenery—he or she wants to focus on, or emphasize. Directors, like painters, compose shots for maximum audience effect. They use visual elements to force the viewer to notice certain areas in a shot.

The most obvious way to focus the viewer's attention is through size—the bigger the object inside the frame, the more likely it will be noticed. How prominently objects will appear onscreen is determined in large part by how far the camera is from the framed area. A herd of elephants filmed from an airplane will appear small within the frame, while a housefly shot from a few inches away will look huge.

Depending on placement, the camera can produce either a long shot, medium shot, or close-up.

A long shot corresponds roughly to the view an audience would get if the action were being presented on a theater stage. All of the actors and their immediate surroundings are visible. A full shot is a type of long shot in which the actor's body is seen in full, with the head near the top of the frame and the feet near the bottom. An extreme long shot is photographed from a great distance and is usually of an outside or exterior location.

Medium shots reveal a moderate amount of visual information. A medium shot of an actor would show the body from the knees or waist up. Close-ups give a detailed view of an object, with little information about its surroundings. A close-up of an actor usually includes only the head. In an extreme close-up, only part of the actor's face—usually the eyes or mouth—are visible.

The same action filmed from different distances will have a different impact on the audience.

Generally, the closer the view (the larger that objects appear on the screen) the more intimate the feel. Close-ups of eyes are especially intense, as the eyes are the body part that express the deepest emotions. Long shots, on the other hand, tend to be neutral. They are more informational than emotional.

POSITION

Like size, directors can use the placement of subjects within the frame to create emphasis. How directors position actors in a shot is particularly important to film composition.

Human faces, with their range of expressions, are natural focal points for viewers, and filmmakers have developed rules regarding their positioning. According to these rules, the strongest visual emphasis is achieved when the actor faces the camera directly. A quarter turn in either direction is somewhat weaker. A half turn, or profile shot, is even weaker. A 180-turn so that the actor's back is to the camera is the weakest of all.

Actors positioned in the foreground, or front, of a shot are stronger than actors placed in background. Although directors rarely put actors dead center in the frame, placing them near the center adds emphasis. Audiences who normally read writing left to right tend to "read" pictures the same way. Consequently, subjects on the left side of the screen are noticed before subjects on the right. (Some languages, such as Chinese and Hebrew, are read

19

either from bottom to top, or right to left, and have a different visual orientation.)

Emphasis can also be achieved through separation and height. An actor standing apart from a group will draw attention, especially if he or she is on the left side of the frame. Similarly, a standing actor will attract more attention than a seated actor placed alongside him or her. An actor standing in the far background of a shot, however, will be less noticeable than a seated actor in the foreground because the seated actor will appear to be "taller" than the standing actor.

ANGLES

Any shot can be enhanced by angle. In eye-level shots, the camera lens is placed parallel to the ground (not tilting), between five and six feet up. Eye-level shots approximate the way an average observer would take in an area and are therefore considered realistic and neutral. The majority of shots are filmed at eye-level.

Other angles include bird's-eye view, high angle, low angle, and oblique angle. Bird's-eye angles are shot from directly overhead, while high-angle shots are less extreme. As the name suggests, a bird's-eye angle allows the audience to view the subject as though watching from a distant perch. Like bird's-eye shots, high-angle shots tend to diminish the importance of the subject because the audience is literally looking down on the subject.

The opposite effect occurs with low-angle shots. In a low-angle shot, the subject is photographed from below and appears to dominate the frame. Low angles are often used to suggest a subject's power and force. Oblique angles are achieved by tilting the camera laterally in order to make the photographed subject appear tilted. Oblique angles create tension and confusion in the viewer and are often used in violent action scenes.

In addition to camera placement, a director can manipulate the viewer's attention through lighting, color, and camera lens choice. Most directors leave the specifics of lighting and lens choices to the cinematographer, and color and décor choices to the production designer. The director, however, oversees the overall look of the film.

THE LOOK

Before shooting begins, the director and cinematographer will come up with a general lighting scheme for the movie, one that reflects the type of story being told. Lighting strategies are executed primarily during shooting, but can be enhanced in post-production.

The three main lighting schemes are high key, low key, and high contrast. Like the mid-day sun, high-key lights flood the setting with bright, shadowless illumination. High-key lighting is often used in comedies or whenever a feeling of openness and optimism is desired. Low-key lighting creates shadows and soft boundaries and is found in many mysteries and horror stories. With high-contrast light, the boundaries between light and dark areas appear sharp. High-contrast lighting works well in dramas, especially ones with strong, opposing characters.

Most movies utilize both theatrical and available light. Theatrical lights vary in size and intensity and are used on sets as well as on location. Available light is light that occurs naturally in a setting. Usually, this is outdoor light, but it can also come from house lamps, candles, or any source of illumination normally found at a given location.

Available lighting maximizes the realism of a scene, while theatrical lighting makes a more deliberate dramatic statement. Any lighting scheme can be augmented through the use of camera filters. Usually made of glass or plastic, filters are placed over the camera lens and can intensify or soften light. Some filters sharpen the contrast between dark and light colors, while others blur or diffuse the contrast.

Within specific shots, the director can use light to lead the viewer toward a certain subject in the frame. Like a spotlight in the theater, photographic lighting can zero in on an object and thereby give it literal and symbolic importance.

Bathing a subject in light suggests purity and openness. Likewise, placing part or all of an subject in darkness will make that subject appear mysterious and sinister. For example, in one scene in Francis Ford Coppola's 1972 gangster classic *The Godfather,* Marlon Brando's face was lit with a harsh overhead light that hid his eyes and made him appear especially threatening to the audience.

Directors can combine angle and lighting techniques for even greater effect. In *War of the Worlds* (2005), Steven Spielberg introduced Tim Robbins' Harlan Ogilvy character by shooting him from a low angle and keeping part of his face in shadow. Although the character is not threatening at this point, the shot hints at the danger he will pose later on in the story.

LIGHTING STRATEGIES

Some movie stories inspire directors to come up with a lighting strategy for the entire film. For his 1981 drama, *Prince of the City*, the story of a police detective who gradually uncovers corruption among his fellow officers, Sidney Lumet worked out the following lighting scheme with cinematographer Andrzej Barkowiak:

"In the first third of the movie, we tried to have the light on the background brighter than on the actors in the foreground. For the second third, the foreground light and the background light were more or less balanced. Only the foreground, occupied by the actors, was lit. By the end of the movie, only the relationships that were about to be betrayed mattered. People emerged from the background.

Where something took place no longer mattered. *What* mattered was what took place and to whom."[5]

COLOR

As with lighting, directors can use color to influence how a viewer responds to a subject. Although satisfactory color film stock did not become available until the late 1930s, early filmmakers would often add washes of color during printing to create mood and atmosphere. In D. W. Griffith's 1915 film *The Birth of a Nation*, for example, scenes depicting the burning of Atlanta were printed on red stock, while the love scenes were printed on yellow stock.

Today's movies are often conceived with a color look that matches the film's prevailing mood. The look can be achieved through a combination of lighting techniques, set décor, costumes, makeup, and film-processing. Comedies, outdoor adventures, musicals, and romances often favor warm colors (red, yellow, orange, yellow-green), while thrillers, science fiction, and other dramas are frequently shot with cool colors (blue, blue-green, violet).

For example, Michael Mann's nighttime thriller *Collateral* (2004) has a cool blue look that underscores the mystery of its harsh urban landscape. The historical racing film *Seabiscuit* (2003), on the other hand, emphasizes warm colors.

In the 2004 psychological horror picture *The Village*, colors play an important role, both as symbols and as plot points. Red is the village's forbidden color, as it is associated with the monsters of the forest, while yellow is used by the villagers as a form of protection. In an interview about the film, director M. Night Shyamalan discussed his use of "plot colors": "Red creates agitation. If the room was red we would be agitated and anxious and aggressive. And yellow calms us and placates us and makes us feel safe and more open to things."[6]

As with lighting, directors can also employ color for effect in a specific shot or scene, drawing the viewer's eye to a particular object or person within the frame. For instance, in the musical romance *West Side Story* (1961), when hero Tony first spies the sweet and innocent Maria at a dance, Maria wears a white dress that stands out from the other dancers' clothes in the scene. The viewer's eye is drawn to Maria's dress, just as Tony is drawn to Maria.

Director Sidney Lumet says about color: "Color is highly subjective. Blue or red may mean totally different things to you or me. But as long as my interpretation of a color is consistent, eventually you'll become aware (subconsciously, I hope) of how I'm using that color and what I'm using it for."[7]

LENSES

In addition to moving the camera closer or farther away from a subject, filmmakers can change the framing of a shot through lens choice. Depending on the lens, a filmed subject can appear to be either

M. Night Shyamalan at the New York premiere of his 2006 film Lady in the Water.

near or far away from the viewer, while remaining the same distance from the camera. Directors select lenses based on the dramatic effect they wish to achieve.

Movie lenses range from normal, wide-angle, and telephoto. Because they are the lenses that most closely resembles human sight, normal lenses are the most commonly used. Normal lenses create a natural, realistic look. Wide-angle lenses, on the other hand, allow the camera to photograph a wider area than a normal lens. They exaggerate perspective and create a deep depth of field.

Depth of field, also known as depth of focus, refers to how much of a photographed area, foreground to background, appears in focus. In a deep depth-of-field shot, objects in the background appear as sharply focused as objects in the foreground. Directors often choose deep focus when they want to show simulta-neous back-ground and foreground action within the same shot. One action might complement the other, or it might clash with the other.

> **DEPTH OF FIELD—**
> The distance in front of the camera lens within which objects appear in sharp focus.

Telephoto lenses, also called long lenses, create the opposite effect. They flatten perspective by magnifying the size of objects in the background. Telephoto lenses, which can capture images clearly from a long distance, are useful when filming in crowded locations, or in any situation where the presence of the camera might be intrusive. They allow the filmmaker to make a faraway subject appear close and in focus, while keeping the surroundings blurry.

In an online essay, cinematographer Mark Woods (*The Eliminator*) defined the difference between wide-angle and long lenses this way: "A 25mm [wide-angle] feels like my aunt. She's someone who wants to include all the family at her large house but can be very dramatic when confronted up close and personal. . . .

"An 80mm [long] lens is much like a niece of mine who is very pretty and self-absorbed. Often, she doesn't see beyond the depth of her mirror, and isolates the situations she's confronted with without considering the 'bigger picture.'"[8]

CHANGING FOCUS

Long lenses also permit the filmmaker to change focus during a shot. The camera focuses first on a subject in the foreground then shifts to focus on a subject in the background. This technique, called rack focusing, redirects the viewer's attention from one subject to another without interrupting the flow of the action. Symbolically, it connects the two subjects in the viewer's mind.

In *Ray* (2004), director Taylor Hackford used rack focusing to show the audience how the boy Ray Charles (C. J. Sanders) learned to cope with his blindness by honing his listening skills. Every time young Ray shifts his attention to a new sound in his house, the camera shifts focus from Ray to the source of the sound. Hackford also used rack focusing in many shots to connect Ray, the adult musician (Jamie Foxx), to his onscreen audience.

Zoom lenses allow the cameraman to change from wide angle to telephoto shots in one continuous movement. Zooming can create an effect similar to rack focusing, but with greater range.

THE MOVING CAMERA

Movie pioneer Edwin S. Porter had been making films for only a couple of years when he came up with the idea to shoot part of the short silent *The Great Train Robbery* with a moving camera. Porter's moves were modest in scope, but they represented an important addition to cinematic art.

Pans

The first camera move ever undertaken was a pan. Short for panorama, a pan involves turning the camera horizontally from left to right, or right to left. Usually, the camera is mounted on a tripod and is level with the ground. Like rack focus shots, pans connect subjects within a shot. They can also effectively convey a sense of space, harmony, and grandeur.

As director Martin Scorsese (*Raging Bull*, *The Departed*) observed, one slow pan shot of a mountain valley, for instance, can be more visually powerful than a series of long shots of the same

Director Martin Scorsese at work on the set of his classic film GoodFellas *in 1990.*

vista. "Panning works in location-type situations, a desert or a jungle or a city, where you can pan straight across—start with two characters, pan them out of frame, and you pan across and see other things going by, and you see the entire world and you pan over to something that's going on across the street. You can utilize that in the narrative."[9]

Swish pans are fast horizontal moves that blur the image. Although swish pans, also known as flash or zip pans, connect subjects like a normal pan, they confuse and excite the viewer at the same time.

Tilts and Traveling Shots

In addition to pans, there are three basic camera moves: tilts, traveling shots, and crane shots (including aerial). Tilts are the opposite of pans. Instead of moving side to side, the camera moves up and down like a nodding head. Tilts are most often point-of-view shots—mimicking a character looking up or down. Like pans, tilts can create connections between subjects in a visually suggestive way.

> **POINT-OF-VIEW SHOT (POV)**—A shot approximating the view of a specific character.

For traveling shots, also known as dolly or tracking shots, the camera is placed on a moving vehicle. Usually, the vehicle is a platform with wheels, not unlike a mover's dolly, but the camera can also be mounted on a car, train, horse, bike—anything that goes. For some traveling shots, the camera is pulled along tracks laid on the floor of a film set.

> **TRACKING SHOT**—Usually, a traveling shot for which tracks are laid down for the camera to roll on. Also known as a dolly shot.

Other traveling shots are accomplished with the aid of a Steadicam, a device that enables the camera to shoot smoothly while being held.

A held camera allows for more freedom of movement than a mounted camera. If maximum

Visual Strategies

Below are two examples of how directors used visual tools—framing, angles, movement, and lenses—to achieve very different dramatic results in similar tight settings. In the first example, director Frank Darabont describes how he made the closed set of the prison drama *The Green Mile* (1999) less tedious for the viewer. In the second, director Sidney Lumet details how he created a "sense of entrapment" in the jury room set of *Twelve Angry Men* (1957).

Darabont: "My cinematographer David Tattersall and I really had a lot of discussions about how to keep that cell block set interesting. We wanted very much to approach every scene on that cell block in some kind of visually different manner—whether it was choice of lens in that we would shoot something with long lens versus a wide frame, whether it was a subtle bit of camera movement, whether it was the tone of the lighting, whether it's a sunny day outside or whether it's a cloudy day outside, whether it's nighttime, whether it's daytime. We always wanted to keep it slightly different so that it wouldn't visually oppress the audience."[10]

Lumet: "As the picture unfolded, I wanted the [jury] room to seem smaller and smaller. That meant that I would slowly shift to longer lenses as the picture continued. . . . In addition, I shot the first third of the movie above eye level, and then, by lowering the camera, shot the second third at eye level, and the last third from below eye level. In that way, toward the end, the ceiling began to appear. Not only were the walls closing in, the ceiling was as well. The sense of increasing claustrophobia did a lot to raise the tension of the last part of the movie."[11]

In deciding how to shoot these films, both directors came up with a visual strategy that matched their interpretations of the stories. In *The Green Mile*, Darabont wanted to bring out the humanity and hope of an otherwise inhuman, hopeless situation—death row. He therefore strove to make the prison set as open and changeable as he could.

By contrast, Lumet saw the jury room in *Twelve Angry Men* as a kind of prison, a place where strangers are forced to come together to make difficult decisions. His visual choices, therefore, emphasized the closeness and discomfort of the room.

realism is desired, a director might choose to shoot with a moving hand-held camera.

Directors choose traveling shots for different reasons—some artistic, some practical. Often, traveling shots are designed to maximize a particular point of view—the audience moves through the filmed environment along with the character. The television show *The West Wing* used long tracking shots accompanied by fast-paced dialogue to evoke the nonstop hustle and bustle of the White House.

Traveling shots can also comment symbolically on the action. One of the best-known Steadicam traveling shots can be found in the opening of Scorsese's 1990 film *GoodFellas*. During one three-minute traveling shot, Scorsese followed his protagonist, Henry Hill, as he wound his way through a nightclub filled with friends. The lengthy shot introduced the story's main characters from Henry's point of view, allowing the audience to get an immediate feel for Henry's world.

In a crane shot, the camera is mounted on a crane, similar to those used in building construction. Designed to hold both the camera and the cameraman, cranes allow for moving overhead shots from virtually any angle. Aerial shots are usually taken from a helicopter and offer a broader view than a typical crane shot. Aerial shots often open films, or introduce the audience to a new location.

ELEMENTS OF DIRECTING:
STAGING THE SCENE

While shots are the basic visual unit for the director, scenes are the basic dramatic unit. A film scene consists of a series of shots related to one another by a common setting or related settings. Scenes are sometimes grouped into sequences, larger narrative chunks with a common dramatic goal.

Shots are connected through editing— literally, the joining of one strip of film (one shot) with another. The action depicted in a single edited scene is usually continuous and typically runs between thirty and 120 onscreen seconds (although shorter and longer scenes are not uncommon). In the script itself, scenes are marked by sluglines, shorthand text that describes the place and time of day that the action takes place.

35

POINT OF VIEW

Like the script as a whole, scenes have their own beginnings, middles, and ends, and their own conflicts and resolutions. When planning a scene, directors first determine from whose point of view it is being told. Often the protagonist functions as the point-of-view character, but any character can claim point of view in a given scene.

Point of view can be suggested by which character is emphasized in the script's stage directions—the text that describes the nonspeaking, physical action of a scene. Some scenes might appear to "belong" strongly to one character in the script, like first-person narration in a novel. These first-person scenes have a subjective point of view. Other scenes might be neutral, or objective, in their point of view, not favoring one character over another.

The director will also consider how the scene fits into the whole. How does it advance the story and affect the development of the characters? What should the audience know about the characters at the scene's beginning?

In addition to figuring out the overall purpose of a scene, the director must also determine the objectives of the characters within the scene itself. What are their goals? What do they want? What obstacles do they face?

To understand a scene's objectives, directors sometimes break the text into narrative blocks, bits of action that parallel the scene's dramatic structure. Each block has its own mini-objective and structure. (Some like to think of narrative blocks as being like paragraphs in a chapter of a book.) Narrative blocks help the director pinpoint what is going on in a scene moment by moment.

STAGING THE ACTION

After the script has been broken down and analyzed, the director decides how to stage each scene—what types of shots will best realize the dramatic objectives of each scene. With staging, directors combine *mise-en-scène* and the actors' perform-ances to build a coherent scene out of individual shots.

Staging takes place during principal photography, the period during production when most of the action of a script is filmed. Whether the scene is shot indoors on a set or outdoors on location, the director is supported by a large crew, including camera, lighting, and sound technicians, makeup artists, costumers, set decora-tors, and builders. Each shot

PRINCIPAL PHOTOGRAPHY— The main photography of a film and the period during which it takes place.

requires its own set-up—the positioning of the lights and camera. To save time and money, scenes that occur in the same location are usually filmed together, regardless of where in the script they appear. An opening scene might be shot on the same day as an ending scene.

In addition to rendering the action of a scene, directors can accomplish a number of important tasks through staging.

* First, staging helps define the physical space in which a scene takes place. Unless keeping the viewer in the dark about a location is important to the storytelling, directors will supply enough visual information to reveal where the action is occurring. The audience will also want to know where the actors are in relation to one another and in relation to the space around them.

Through their shot selection, directors help viewers orient themselves in the scene. For example, a long shot of the setting, or establishing shot, conveys the scene's general location. Over-the-shoulder and reverse angle shots, in which an actor is photographed from over the shoulder of another actor, and vice-versa, establish the physical space between actors in dialogue exchanges.

> ESTABLISHING SHOT—A shot that gives the viewer an overview of a scene setting, usually coming at the beginning of a scene.

* Staging is key to establishing point of view in a scene. Viewers instinctively feel point of view through camera placement. Shooting with a hand-held camera, where the camera stands in for a character, produces the most subjective staging. In effect the camera's eye becomes the character's eyes.

More often a subjective point of view is conveyed through less extreme camera placement. In a point-of-view shot (POV) the camera approximates the character's perspective. POV shots temporarily place the audience inside a character's head. Directors will often juxtapose a POV shot with a reverse-angle shot—that is, a shot looking back from the opposite angle. In that way, the audience not only sees what the character sees, but also observes the character's reaction to it.

Sometimes a subjective mood can be created simply by focusing on a particular character, especially when alone. Close-ups are common in such scenes. By getting visually close, the audience begins to identify with the character.

If the director has decided on a neutral or objective point of view for all or part of a scene, the camera becomes like a fly on the wall, registering the action without inviting the viewer to identify with a particular character. Neutral camera placement considers all the performers in a scene, more or less equally. A majority of movie scenes are shot with a neutral camera.

* Staging can also direct the viewer's attention toward a particular object in a scene and highlight certain actions. If all the actors in a scene turn and look to the left, for example, the viewer will assume that something interesting is going on in that direction.

* Through staging, directors can quickly indicate relationships among characters. At the start of *The Godfather*, Don Corleone sits behind his desk in his

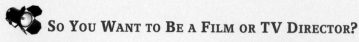

Marlon Brando as Don Corleone in a scene from The Godfather *(1972), as directed by Francis Ford Coppola. Note the heavy shadows around his eyes and mouth caused by the overhead lighting.*

home office while another man, Bonasera (Salvatore Corsitto) speaks to him across the desk. Corleone's son Sonny (James Caan) and his lawyer, Tom Hayden (Robert Duvall), are behind and to the side of Corleone. Corleone's position behind the desk tells the audience that he is the man in charge . . . the boss. The visually weaker position of Sonny and Tom reveals that while they are on Corleone's side (literally and figuratively), they are subordinate to him.

* Staging is another tool for expressing visually what a character is feeling inside. A character who enters a room and begins to pace up and down and look at his watch repeatedly conveys without words impatience and worry.

* Staging can also suggest thematic ideas. Though now a cinematic cliché, directors who want to underline a character's self-sacrifice, for example, will sometimes pose the actor with outstretched "Christ on the Cross" arms. Similarly, a director can suggest purity by staging the scene next to water or having the character wash himself.

COVERAGE

When filming, directors always have to think ahead to the editing room, keeping in mind what visual information will be needed for the scene to cut together properly and make sense to the viewer.

Although experienced directors sometimes forgo them, scenes are often constructed according to a few basic rules of shot selection. This shot selection allows the director to cover a scene by filming all the visual information required for editing.

Traditionally, the first shot taken is the master shot. For a master shot, the contents of the entire scene are filmed in one uninterrupted take (one recording of a shot). Master shots are almost always long or full shots—far enough away from the subjects to show all the action from beginning to end. Master shots are complemented first by medium shots, usually two shots that feature two actors from the waist up, then by single shots (over-the-shoulder and reverse angle) of the actors.

Once a scene has been fully covered in this way, directors will often add other types of shots to make the visual storytelling more interesting. How many shots are taken for each scene depends in part on the budget (the more shots, the more time, the more money), the shooting schedule, and the setting itself.

Many directors, especially experienced ones, replace traditional multi-shot coverage with traveling shots that capture the necessary visual information in one take. The traveling shot might start long, revealing the entire setting, and gradually move in to a close-up.

BLOCKING

In addition to camera moves, directors must plan the movement of actors within a setting. How actors move within a scene is called blocking. As with all other aspects of directing, blocking choices are designed to reflect and enhance the objectives of the scene. A director might prefer to keep the actors in one spot throughout a shot or scene, or have one actor move, while another stays still.

Often, if characters are emotionally close, the director will keep them physically close during a scene. Likewise, if they are estranged, or are strangers, the director will likely put physical distance between them. Walls, doors, fences, furniture, and other props can create symbolic as well as literal barriers within a scene.

In a key scene in the 2004 film biography *The Aviator*, when movie star Katharine Hepburn (Cate Blanchett) breaks up with her reclusive lover Howard Hughes (Leonardo DiCaprio), director Martin Scorsese separated the characters with a closed bedroom door. While touching the door tenderly, Hepburn breaks the news to Hughes that she has met someone new and is leaving him. The door conveys in both a literal and symbolic way the fears that torment Hughes.

Similarly, in a scene in *The Godfather*, during which Don Corleone symbolically passes the family business to his son Michael (Al Pacino), director Coppola arranged the seated actors so that they were almost touching each other, but looking in opposite directions. Coppola's staging expresses both the closeness of the two men and the tension inherent in their relationship.

THAT FACE, THAT VOICE!

Casting of a movie often begins before the first word of a script is written. Sometimes writers will create a part with a particular actor in mind, or a director reading a script for the first time will picture a favorite actor in a given role. More often than not, a different

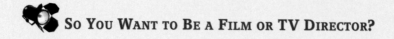

actor will actually end up in the part, but these initial mental suggestions are the first step in casting.

Director Barry Levinson (*Diner*, *Rain Man*) described the casting process this way: "Casting is always an interesting process, because you need a certain kind of blend of characters, or actors who have different kinds of rhythms and define things in a certain kind of way. Especially with an ensemble cast, you really have to put together a little music group, in a way."[1]

Director Barry Levinson (seated, second from left) watches film with some of the cast and crew of Envy *(2004).*

Frank Darabont says about casting: "For me, the casting process is usually a fairly straightforward one. I have actors in and read the pages . . . there's usually one who matches whatever picture you have in your head for that role. There's always one who feels right for the part. . . . What I expect any actor to bring to a project—aside from their talent, which can be a considerable blessing—is a belief in the material."[2]

According to veteran TV director Lee Shallat Chemel (*Murphy Brown, Gilmore Girls*), "You start to feel character elements when you read the script and you hear the voices. The first thing you do is you think of actors you've known whose voice would be right. . . . You work with a casting person. You'll mention other actors as types, you'll mention physical characteristics, especially if they're required in the screenplay. . . . You do everything you can to hit the facets that are in your imagination. Then you begin to see actors do the lines. And that changes everything. Because some will have a completely different take on it that you love. . . . Actors have always changed my view about what a part can be."[3]

WORKING WITH ACTORS

Acting is the one element of directing where the director's control is limited. The director can plan each shot down to the inch and execute it with great precision on the set, but he or she cannot force an actor to deliver a convincing performance. Nor can the director create a great performance in the editing room. Consequently, being able to work with actors is an all-important skill for a director.

Every actor has his or her own method for bringing a character to life. Some actors base their impersonations on people they know. Some find physical qualities to work from—an accent, a costume, makeup, or a prop. Others dissect the character's emotional background and look for similar experiences in their own lives to inspire their performance.

Shallat Chemel described her growth as an actors' director this way: "In the beginning of my career, I felt what the director had to do was control the actor's performance and make it happen the way you see it. That was arrogance and ignorance on my part. You have to really watch what an actor is bringing you . . . let the actor inform you in the directing."[4]

According to Shallat Chemel, the goal of the director is to create a relationship with the actor: "to feel the character is alive in that actor . . . and to find the chemistry between the characters who have relationships in the film."[5] For Shallat Chemel, a good performance happens only when the actor has convincingly wrapped himself in the world of the film. "The director has to create the context for acting in such a specific way. . . . For example, to say: 'In this scene, it's important for the audience to ascertain that this man is about to explode, but the character

THE 180-DEGREE RULE

Few movie viewers would be able to explain the 180-degree rule, but most would know if it had been broken. The rule helps viewers orient themselves visually and understand the layout of a setting. Briefly, the rule states that whenever there are two subjects (A and B) within a filmed space, an imaginary line, called the axis, runs between them.

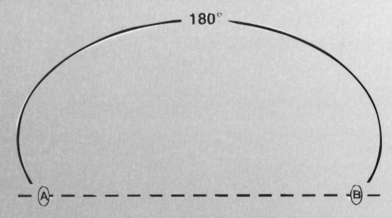

If the camera is moved, as in medium or close-up shots, stationary subjects must appear consistently either to the left or right of the camera during the entire scene. To maintain consistency, the camera must stay on the same side of the imaginary line throughout the scene. If the camera crosses the line, the subjects will appear to have flipped to the other side of the frame after the shots are edited together. On rare occasions, filmmakers will deliberately "jump the line," or violate the 180-degree rule, for dramatic effect.

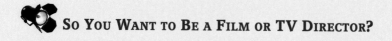

must never think he's revealing he's about to explode.' The director won't say how to do that."[6]

Each director has his or her own method for working with actors. Some like to rehearse extensively and allow the actors to talk out their parts before shooting. Others prefer to jump into filming and let the actors discover their characters' rhythms and quirks on their own. Some directors require actors to stick closely to the script; others encourage improvisation, inventing as they go along. Regardless of methodology, a good director knows how to work with all types of actors and can bring the best out in their performances.

ELEMENTS OF DIRECTING:
POST-PRODUCTION

Once a film is shot and "in the can" it goes into post-production, the final step in the artistic process. Post-production starts in the editing room and includes music scoring, sound editing and dubbing, and print preparation. To a greater or lesser extent, the director is involved in all of these processes.

EDITING BASICS

Of the various post-production activities, editing is the one on which the director typically spends the most time. Some directors, like Steven Spielberg and M. Night Shyamalan, are known for "editing in the camera." That is, for planning and shooting their scenes so carefully that little editorial decision-making is required in post-production. For most directors, however, the editing room represents a key third step in the creation of a movie.

As with staging, editing serves multiple purposes. A majority of editing is done to achieve continuity— that is, the edited shots are put together logically and render the action more or less realistically. "Cutting to continuity" simply means that the cuts are smooth and any reduction of time and space is unnoticeable. A scene depicting a woman crossing a parking lot and opening a car door, for instance, might start with a long shot showing the woman walking up to the car, then cut to a closer shot of her arm reaching for the door handle. If cut properly, the viewer will not be aware that a few moments of the action have been cut out to save screen time.

In classic editing, pioneered by D. W. Griffith in the 1910s, coverage footage is cut together to make continuity easy. The long master shot (establishing shot) introduces the setting at the beginning of a scene. Medium shots of the actors, including two shots and over-the-shoulder and reverse-angle shots, come next, followed by close-ups.

As the scene progresses, the director will go back and forth between medium and close-up shots and may return to the establishing shot. The goal of the "Griffith formula," as it is sometimes called, is to bring the viewer into the scene as clearly and quickly as possible.

Cross-cutting and Beyond

In 1903, Edwin S. Porter's *The Great Train Robbery* revolutionized movies by introducing parallel action and cross-cutting to the film narrative. Parallel action allowed the audience to follow two separate story lines at once—the train robbery in one location and the posse formation in another. Porter accomplished parallel action through cross-cutting, an editing technique in which shots from one setting are put next to shots from another setting.

> **CROSS-CUTTING—** The alternating of shots from two sequences, usually in different locations, to suggest the action is going on at the same time.

Another form of editing is called thematic editing. The father of thematic editing was Russian filmmaker Sergei Eisenstein. In the 1920s, Eisenstein declared that montage, or editing, was the foundation of all moviemaking. He saw montage not just as a way to increase tension and excitement, but as a vital storytelling tool in its own right.

> **MONTAGE—**Film editing, particularly editing in which images are connected thematically.

Rather than starting with a master long shot and cutting to closer shots, Eisenstein juxtaposed, or put together, shots of different subjects, often close-ups, to create a whole new meaning. Eisenstein believed that when one shot is put together with another, with each shot having its own dramatic meaning, a third, separate meaning, or idea, results.

A scene from the classic "Odessa steps" sequence in The Battleship Potemkin *(1925), directed by Sergei Eisenstein.*

In his 1925 silent classic *The Battleship Potemkin*, Eisenstein used his editorial techniques to dramatize the real-life story of military rebellion and unrest in the Russian town of Odessa. More than just depicting the uprising through action, Eisenstein juxtaposed shots that suggested symbolically the *idea* of rebellion.

In one scene, for example, Eisenstein cut together quick shots of three lion statues, each one in a different pose. The editing made it appear as though a single lion were waking up and rising to attention, just as the sailors and townspeople were symbolically waking and rising up against their oppressors. Separately, the lions suggested one thing; strung together, they implied something completely different.

Although Eisenstein's editing techniques were heavy-handed by today's standards, they nevertheless revolutionized the way filmmakers approached montage. Today's directors often combine editing techniques for maximum effect. For example in the ending of *The Godfather*, director Coppola intercut shots of Michael Corleone participating in his godchild's christening ceremony with shots of the brutal slayings of his gangster rivals. The action within each scene is cut realistically to continuity, but by cross-cutting between the two seemingly unrelated activities, Coppola suggests thematically the duality and hypocrisy of Michael's new life as a mafia don.

IN THE EDITING ROOM

Editing a film involves several steps. During or immediately after shooting, editors and their assistants assemble the raw footage in chronological order of the story. The director watches the assembled footage, choosing which takes of a shot he or she prefers. The editor then removes the selected takes and cuts them together according to the director's original shot order. Takes that are not selected are called outtakes.

From this initial assembly the director begins to shape the footage into a rough cut. With guidance from the editor, the director screens the footage scene by scene to determine the effectiveness of the shot selection and structure. As it is put together, the director asks: Is the scene clear? Is the coverage adequate? Does the scene advance the story? Are the performances convincing? If necessary, the director can change the order of scenes, or re-edit a scene to change point of view or dramatic emphasis.

Once the film's scene-by-scene structure has been worked out, the director begins to polish and tighten. This last stage of picture editing is called the fine cut. The primary concern of the fine cut is to adjust the tempo, or pace, of the movie.

Rhythm and Tempo

Eisenstein was not only expert at juxtaposition, he also understood the importance of tempo in editing. Eisenstein was the first director to cut a scene to the beats of a music score, and his editing was known for its rhythmic precision. Although it is rare today to cut films to match a musical score, directors are nonetheless keenly aware of tempo when they are overseeing the editing of a picture.

Some shots, like long traveling shots, set their own tempo. Most shots, however, must be cut with others to achieve the desired tempo. In *Making Movies*, Lumet noted that "The more cuts, the faster the tempo will seem."[1] The famous shower scene in Alfred Hitchcock's *Psycho* (1960) contains a whopping number of edits, one for every half-second of film. The rapid-fire editing makes the scene feel especially frenzied, much more so than if it had been shot in one long take.

In addition to fixing the tempo for each scene, the director has to be aware of the overall tempo of the film, the scene-to-scene rhythm. A thirty-second television commercial can be cut to the same tempo (usually fast), but not a full-length feature film. Lumet notes that "if a picture is edited in the same tempo for its entire length, it will *feel* much longer. It doesn't matter if five cuts per minute or five cuts every ten minutes are being used. . . . In other words, it's the *change* in tempo that we feel, not the tempo itself."[2]

Transitions

For extra emphasis, directors sometimes use simple effects—fade-ins, fade-outs, and dissolves—when transitioning between scenes. A fade-in is the slow brightening of the image from blackness to normal lighting. A fade-out reverses the process, from light to dark. Directors use fade-ins and fade-outs at the beginning and end of a picture, or between scenes, usually to indicate a jump in time and/or setting.

In a dissolve, one image fades out slowly while the next image fades in slowly. Halfway through, the two images become superimposed—that is, for a second or two, both images appear on the screen at the same time. Like fades, dissolves can indicate a

Director Alfred Hitchcock and actor Anthony Perkins (left to right) on the set of Hitchcock's 1960 film, Psycho.

jump in time, but usually suggest a stronger connection between one scene and the next than a fade.

The Soundtrack

No element of filmmaking is less appreciated and more misunderstood than sound. With the addition of sound—dialogue, music, and noises—movies achieved new cinematic heights.

Filmmakers actually began producing short sound movies as early as 1900. Over the next twenty-five years, various sound-recording techniques were tried with limited success. The movie that finally launched the "talking pictures" phenomenon was Warner Bros.' 1927 feature *The Jazz Singer*. Although not the first film to include some synchronized dialogue and singing—sounds that synchronize or match up with the images—*The Jazz Singer* wrapped the innovation up in an appealing package that wowed audiences.

Movie sound can be divided into three major groups: sound effects, music, and language, usually dialogue. Sound can be synchronous, or non-synchronous—sound that is detached from the visuals, like background music. Most dialogue is synchronized, although typically at least some dialogue is rerecorded, or dubbed, in the studio. Sound effects include natural and mechanical noises, such as explosions, revving engines, animal cries, rain, and sighs. All these sound components are combined in the studio to produce a soundtrack that is joined with the image track.

As they do with cinematographers and production designers, directors often confer with sound designers before, during, and after production. The sound designer and director work together to plan a consistent approach to the movie's soundtrack.

One of the industry's most distinguished sound designers, Walter Murch (*Apocalypse Now*, *The Godfather II*), stated in an online interview that "emotion, story, and rhythm—apply to sound just as much as they apply to picture. You are always primarily looking for something that will underline or emphasize or counterpoint the emotion that you want to elicit from the audience. You can do that through sound just as well as through editing, if not more so."[3]

Murch offers the presence of background train noises in *The Godfather* as an example of movie sound's emotional impact. Although trains are not seen in the film, they are heard on the soundtrack. "Because there's nothing in the picture that is anything like a train," Murch notes, "the emotion that comes along with that sound, which is a screeching effect as a train turns a difficult corner, gets immediately applied to Michael's state of mind. Here is a person who is also screeching as he turns a difficult corner. This is the first time he is going to kill somebody face to face. He's doing what he said he would never do."[4]

Murch and director Francis Ford Coppola employed the same sound technique to even greater effect in the Vietnam War story *Apocalypse Now* (1979). The terror of the war is represented in the film by a single sound—whirring helicopters. After the movie's release, the sound of helicopters became almost synonymous with the Vietnam conflict.

MUSIC

Like photography and sound effects, music is yet another filmmaking element that directors can manipulate for effect. According to Sidney Lumet, "Almost every picture is improved by a good musical score. To start with, music is a quick way to reach people emotionally."[5]

A few scores consist solely of non-original music—music, often popular songs, written before the film. Director Stanley Kubrick used only non-original orchestral music for his memorable *2001: A Space Odyssey* (1968) score. Some movie scores, like that for *Star Wars* (1977), are wholly original, with every note being composed just for the film. Other films, like *Garden State* (2004), use a combination of original and non-original music.

Movie composers usually enter the production process after filming is done and, as a general rule, write their scores very quickly. Prior to beginning work, a composer will discuss the film with the director to figure out what type of music he or she has imagined for the story. Just as they do for the film's overall look, directors usually have broad,

So You Want to Be a Film or TV Director?

A scene from Stanley Kubrick's groundbreaking special-effects wonder, 2001: A Space Odyssey (1968).

thematic ideas for the score. For a historical film, they might want representative music from the period. For an urban crime story, they might request a jazzy sound, and so on.

Director Lumet described how he works with composers: "[We] sit and talk in order to decide the critical question: What function should the score serve? How can it contribute to the basic question of 'What is the picture about?' We look at the movie reel by reel. I give the composer my feelings about where I think music is necessary, and he does the same. This provides us with a preliminary sketch. Now we review it carefully. Does he have enough room to state the musical ideas clearly? If a musical transition has to take place, have we allowed enough room for it?"[6]

For Lumet and other directors, good scores are "invisible." They add a layer to the drama but never call attention to themselves.

DIRECTING FOR TELEVISION

Although movies and television began development around the same time, television remained a novelty until the late 1940s. The first variety show in the U.S. was telecast in May 1946, and the first continuing drama—a soap opera called *Faraway Hill*—began broadcasting in October 1946. Primetime drama and comedy shows soon followed. Within a few short years, television-viewing became as popular as moviegoing.

The first TV shows were broadcast live—that is, they were viewed more or less at the same time as they were being performed. Even commercials were telecast live in the early days. From the start, directors were essential for a smooth and entertaining broadcast.

TELEVISION VS. MOVIES

With the exception of news and sports, television shows today are rarely broadcast live. The specific duties of the TV director, however, can differ greatly depending on the type of show. Dramas, including one-hour series, movies-of-the-week, and mini-series, are almost always filmed using a single camera, just like feature films. Their crews resemble feature crews, and they may be shot on location, or in a studio, just like features.

Although the television director is the boss on the set, he or she has less control over the content of the script than most movie directors. Series directors are hired on a show-by-show basis and have little involvement in the development of the story lines. Many feature directors write their own scripts, or are able to brainstorm ideas with the screenwriter. Television directors, on the other hand, are given scripts in which the characters, dialogue style, and plot points are more or less fixed.

Television shows also have their own visual and acting style that the director must adhere to. The visual and editing style of *CSI*, with its views of internal organs and other photographic effects, is very different from the style of *Law and Order*, for example. Broad comic acting is the standard on *Scrubs* while *Desperate Housewives* favors a more natural style. Whatever the particular requirements of the show, the series director is expected to stage scenes accordingly.

Budgets and shooting schedules for television shows are usually tighter than those of features. Most feature directors would be happy to get through a page and a half of a script in a day. Commercial directors take two to three days to film thirty seconds. Even on bigger budget shows like *The Sopranos*, TV directors, on the other hand, are expected to shoot anywhere from six to ten pages a day.

The Season One cast of the hit series The Sopranos. *This HBO series was created in a fashion resembling feature filmmaking more so than standard serial television. Still, its televison schedule demanded a greater, faster output of work.*

Consequently, TV directors have less time to finesse a shot or perfect a performance. Their sets are a little less lavish and their post-production resources are more modest. Rehearsal time may be nonexistent, so TV directors prefer to work with experienced actors who can jump into a scene with little preparation.

Visuals

Because of tight production schedules, TV scripts tend to be talkier than movie scripts. It takes considerably more time to shoot an action scene, which requires complex camera moves and many set-ups, than to shoot a scene in which the actors are talking. Telling the story through dialogue rather than action makes filming faster and cheaper, but it also impacts the types of shots a director uses.

Although television screens have gotten bigger over the years, their aspect ratio (width vs. height) is still smaller than the average movie screen. A conventional television screen is narrower and boxier than a movie theater screen (4:3 as compared to 1.85:1). In addition, a typical TV screen displays only about ninety percent of the total filmed image. The edges of the TV image are cut off on many screens; in some cases, more on one side than the other. Consequently, when composing static shots for television, directors stage action more toward the center of the screen than the edges.

Despite its limitations, many feature directors, including Quentin Tarantino and David Lynch (*Twin Peaks*, *Mulholland Drive*), have chosen to work on television. A few, like Spielberg, got their start working in television.

TV COMEDY

In the 1960s and early 1970s, most comedy shows, including *Bewitched* and *Gilligan's Island*, were shot with a single camera. A dubbed laugh track, called "canned laughter," was added later. In 1971, the hit show *All in the Family* changed the way comedies were filmed for television. Like its groundbreaking 1950s predecessor, *I Love Lucy*, *All in the Family* was filmed in front of a studio audience so that live (and therefore more natural-sounding) laughter could be recorded. The 1970s show, however, was shot on videotape, not film, and was not broadcast live but was edited like a single-camera show.

The *All in the Family* model quickly became standard on network television. Studios also began filming two performances of the script each week. Later in the editing room, the best takes of each joke would be culled and spliced together into one continuous performance.

Today, only a few comedy shows, like *Scrubs*, *My Name Is Earl,* and *The Office*, are single-camera shows. The rest are filmed in a studio with a live audience, using four cameras.

The original cast of the landmark television series All in the Family, *featuring (clockwise from top left) Rob Reiner, Sally Struthers, Mike Evans, Carroll O'Connor, and Jean Stapleton.*

DIRECTING THE SITCOM

Four-camera sitcoms—so called because their story lines revolve around a comic situation—have their own directing rules. Photography in multi-camera shows is restricted to capturing the actors' performance on a set. Some special angles and movement are possible, but most scenes consist of static long and medium shots. The point of view is almost always neutral, and little attempt is made to hide the staginess of the presentation.

According to Lee Shallat Chemel, "Sitcoms are a hybrid of stage and film because the actors have to do the whole thing at once [like the stage], but they only get a couple days of rehearsals and you have to shoot it with all your coverage at once."[1]

Sitcom directors also have to think up some of the physical action that goes on in a scene. If the script calls for two characters in a laundromat to notice each other and strike up a conversation, the director will find activities the actors can engage in (buying laundry soap, loading the washer, etc.) to bring them together in the right spot.

"The bulk of direction with comedy," Shallat Chemel notes, "is rhythm, having the actors achieve rhythm so the jokes pop. You have to hear the music of the humor."[2] To achieve rhythm, the sitcom director carefully works out staging in advance. He or she then rehearses the actors on the set so that the jokes are delivered in the right spot at the right time, looking in the right direction, according to the

STORYBOARDS

To communicate visual ideas to the cinematographer and production designer, many feature and TV directors will create storyboards for some or all of the script. Storyboards are sketches of individual shots. Often they describe a series of shots, depicting the action of an entire scene, but they can also describe a single shot. Some productions will hire an artist to draw storyboards for the director. As long as they convey the director's intentions, however, it is not necessary for storyboards to be polished works of art.

Director Chris Wedge reviews the storyboards of his animated film, Ice Age *(2002).*

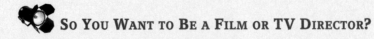

staging. In essence, the sitcom director choreographs the actors with the cameras.

Staging for four-cameras is precise and intricate. Each camera is given a different assignment. One camera—usually near center stage—records the entire scene in a master shot. The other cameras are on the sides, picking up reaction shots and close-ups. The scripts are performed one scene at a time, with all four cameras running simultaneously. Usually, each scene is performed more than once. Retakes—film do-overs—are common, even though the audience has already heard the jokes and seen the comic bits. Later the director will edit the footage from the four cameras, matching the actors' movements to the camera angles.

PUTTING IT ALL TOGETHER:
CITIZEN KANE

In the one-hundred-plus-year-old history of cinema, no movie has garnered as much attention and praise as the 1941 RKO Radio release *Citizen Kane*. Although not a box-office hit, the film wowed critics of the day, made many ten-best lists, and earned several Academy Award nominations. *The New York Times* reviewer Bosley Crowther said after viewing the movie: "*Citizen Kane* is far and away the most surprising and cinematically exciting motion picture to be seen here in many a moon. As a matter of fact, it comes close to being the most sensational film ever made in Hollywood."[1]

Over the decades, *Citizen Kane* has maintained its reputation as the most influential sound movie of all time. Film historian Ephraim Katz described the film as: "A screen work whose inventive construction and innovative cinematographic and sound techniques have greatly influenced filmmakers in America and elsewhere."[2] In 1988, the Library of Congress selected the film as one of the first entrants into the National Film Registry. In 1998, in an industry-wide poll conducted by the American Film Institute, *Citizen Kane* was voted the greatest American movie ever made.

Amazingly, the film's director, co-writer, and star, Orson Welles (1915–1985), was only twenty-five years old when he made the picture, the very first feature of his career. Before movies, Welles had worked in broadcasting—producing, directing, writing, and/or starring in numerous radio dramas. His most famous radio show was an adaptation of H. G. Welles' *The War of the Worlds*, broadcast on Halloween, 1938. Welles' depiction of the alien invasion was so convincing that some listeners believed it was actually happening and started a panic.

Welles, the "boy wonder," came to Hollywood in 1939, and a year later, while under contract at RKO, began work on *Citizen Kane*. The film's title character, Charles Foster Kane, was inspired in part by the real-life William Randolph Hearst, the most powerful newspaper publisher of the day. Angered by Welles' unflattering portrayal of him and his mistress, movie star Marion Davies, Hearst tried to buy all prints of the picture from RKO. He also prohibited the film from being advertised, or even mentioned, in any of his newspapers.

Hearst's attempts to stop the movie's release failed, however, and the film went on to make cinema history.

THE STORY

In addition to its groundbreaking visual and sound elements, the narrative structure of *Citizen Kane* was also unusual for its time. The story of Charles Foster Kane (Orson Welles) is told largely in flashbacks. These flashbacks unfold through the interviews conducted by a reporter assigned to uncover the mystery behind Kane's dying word, "Rosebud." The reporter interviews Kane's best friend, Jedediah Leland (Joseph Cotten); his ex-wife (Dorothy Comingore); and editor, Bernstein (Everett Sloane). Each interview becomes a flashback, with some events described from two different perspectives.

THE LEGEND

At just under two hours, *Citizen Kane* packs a lot of story into a tight package. Every shot in the black-and-white film is artfully constructed, and no screen time is wasted. Each artistic element of the film, from the spare, silent credits, to the fake newsreel, serves to tell the story in the most dramatically effective manner possible.

Orson Welles in a scene from Citizen Kane *(1941).*

The movie is particularly admired for its imaginative visual style, including its stunning deep-focus shots, its use of shadows and low-key lighting, its elaborate camera movements and long takes, and its many dissolves and wipes. Welles found his style with help from veteran cinematographer Gregg Toland, who acted as Welles' photography teacher throughout the production.

In a contemporary article in *American Cinematographer*, Toland explained how he and Welles devised *Citizen Kane* "in such a way that the audience would feel it was looking at reality, rather than merely at a movie."[3] Together, they planned scenes so that "the camera could pan or dolly from one angle to another . . . or so that action which ordinarily would be shown in direct cuts would be shown in a single, longer scene."[4]

Welles and Toland ordered that ceilings be built for the majority of their sets and planned "unusually low camera-setups, so that we could shoot upward and take advantage of the more realistic effects of those ceilings."[5] Until *Citizen Kane,* ceilings were rarely seen in American movies.

Welles, the radio veteran, also used sound in a way that was striking for the time. In his hands, the soundtrack took on a life of its own, sometimes underlining the visuals, sometimes offering its own commentary. Film historian Giannetti observed about the film's soundtrack: "High-angle shots often feature accompanying high pitched music and sound effects; low angles, brooding and low-pitched sounds. . . . Sounds can fade in and out, like images. Sounds can be dissolved and overlapped like images in a montage sequence."[6]

SHOT-BY-SHOT ANALYSIS

Sequence One—Welcome to Xanadu

The twenty-shot opening of *Citizen Kane* is one of the most famous in cinema history. The dramatic objective of the two-block sequence is to introduce the audience to the strange, lonely world of Charles Foster Kane. Only one word is spoken in the entire sequence, but it is the word that propels the rest of the story.

Block One

The first block of the sequence unfolds as a series of dissolves, starting with a medium close shot of a No Trespassing sign affixed to a tall wire fence. It is night, almost dawn. Fog swirls through the air. Playing ominously underneath the visuals is Bernard Herrmann's eerie score. The camera pans slowly up the fence and dissolves first into a shot of another fence, then into a shot of a massive wrought-iron gate.

Shot three dissolves into a view of the top of gate, which is decorated with a huge letter K. In the far background of the shot a castle-like mansion can be seen, perched on top of a craggy hill. Barely visible inside the Xanadu mansion is a single light.

76

Over the next few dissolves, the mansion on the hill appears closer and closer. In the foreground of each shot are the ruins of Xanadu—wild animal cages, a golf course, gondolas on a moat—all empty and falling apart.

Shots eight through ten bring the mansion even closer. The light, which can now be seen shining behind an ornate, diamond-patterned window, dominates the frame. Suddenly, as the music thumps, the light goes out.

Block Two

Shot eleven, a long shot, is taken from inside the mansion, on the other side of the tall window. Replacing the electric light is the natural light of dawn. A tall, canopied bed can be glimpsed in the darkness beneath the window.

As that shot dissolves into the next, flakes of snow fill the screen. Another dissolve reveals a snow-covered cottage, nestled in a wintry landscape. Abruptly, the camera pulls back to reveal that the cottage is actually inside a glass globe. A man's hand, in close-up, is shown holding the globe. The "snow" continues to fall across the frame.

Shot fourteen is an extreme close-up of the man's lips, whispering the word "Rosebud." In the following shot, the man's limp arm releases the globe, which rolls down two carpeted stairs to the floor. In shot sixteen, the globe breaks on the marble floor, sending glass and water spraying. The music thuds in unison with the break.

The iconic snowglobe in a pivotal early scene of Citizen Kane.

The next two shots are taken at floor level, the image refracted through a piece of the broken glass. A nurse is seen opening the bedroom door and hurrying into the room. The image is odd and distorted.

In shot nineteen, the nurse bends over the bed and gently places the man's hands on his chest. As the camera pans across the man's body, the nurse pulls the sheet over his face. The final shot returns to the long view of the bed and fades to black.

Whose scene is it? The scene is Kane's. Even in death Kane and his Xanadu dominate.

What is the objective of the sequence?

The opening sequence introduces the audience to the film's protagonist and sets the drama in motion.

The Whole Package

Welles accomplishes a lot in the opening. First, he sets the tone for the film. Fog effects and spooky music create a feeling of mystery and foreboding. Immediately, the audience senses that something dramatic is about to happen.

Second, Welles gives the audience some key information about the arena in which the film takes place. By starting at the outer edge of Xanadu—the No Trespassing sign—and moving slowly in and up to the mansion, the grand vastness of Xanadu is conveyed. The audience knows that they are entering an eccentric, lavish world.

Third, the scene previews what will be the emotional core of the drama. As designed and shot, Xanadu appears to be a lonely prison. The No Trespassing sign and the criss-crosses of the wire fences and window panes are both literal and symbolic barriers. They tell the viewer that the mansion's occupant is a recluse, that he wants to keep the outside world at bay. The empty animal cages and rundown golf course suggest loss and loneliness, as does the one light shining in the otherwise dark mansion.

Block two of the opening sequence accomplishes a different goal—the creation of a mystery. Instead of trying to orient the audience in the setting, Welles' staging deliberately makes the interior of Kane's bedroom shadowy. He does the same with Kane. The first view the audience gets of the man is an extreme close-up of his lips saying the word "Rosebud." His face is never shown in full.

By focusing on the globe, especially the drifting "snow," Welles then brings the viewer right into the mind of the dying Kane. The shots are highly subjective, as though seen and felt by Kane himself. Although at this point they cannot know why, the audience understands that the globe, like the word "Rosebud," is going to be an important detail in the story.

The broken globe shots hint at the reflective nature of the drama—Kane's story is about to be told, but through others, refracted through other people's memories and emotions. The arrival of the nurse is a last bit of telling information for the audience—Kane has died without family or friends, alone and in the shadows.

Though less than three minutes long, the sequence delivers a lot of information and feeling. Welles returns to this same Xanadu setting at the very end of the picture. After the Rosebud sled burns in the furnace—revealing to the audience the significance of Kane's last word—the camera moves outward, in reverse of the opening. Fittingly the final shot of the movie is of the No Trespassing sign.

SEQUENCE TWO—"YOU'RE FIRED!"

About two-thirds of the way into *Citizen Kane* comes another outstanding scene. A final part of Jed Leland's flashback, the nighttime scene takes place at the *Chicago Inquirer* city room after the singing debut of Kane's second wife, Susan Alexander.

Block One

The first shot of the scene is a medium shot taken from inside the city room. From a brightly lit hallway, Kane enters through a set of glass doors. It is after hours, and the room is dimly lit. Offscreen, Bernstein and another *Inquirer* editor are heard discussing Susan's debut. Unnoticed Kane hides in semi-darkness, listening as the junior editor gives Bernstein a rundown on the post-show press.

In shot two, a full shot, Bernstein is seen in the foreground huddled with the editor and a group of reporters. Bernstein continues to question the men until Kane steps from the shadows, startling them. Bernstein tells Kane that all the reviews are ready to go, except for the "dramatic" review, which Leland is still writing.

After a long pause, Kane moves right, and the camera pans with him, revealing Leland's office in the far background. As Kane strides back to the office, Bernstein, near the foreground, nervously explains to the others that Kane and Leland have not spoken to each other in years. Bernstein then follows Kane into the office. All areas of the frame remain sharp in this deep focus shot.

Block Two

The first shot of block two takes place in Leland's office. Leland is passed out over his typewriter, his bottle of alcohol next to him on the desk. In the next shot, Kane is shown standing on the other side of the desk. Shots four through fourteen then go back and forth between the two men as they talk over Leland's slumped body.

On Kane's order, Bernstein reluctantly reads outloud what Leland has typed, including his description of Susan as a "hopelessly incompetent amateur." When Bernstein stops in mid-sentence, Kane rips the paper out of the typewriter and chuckles tensely as he reads what Leland has written. Kane completes Leland's thought, saying that Susan's acting "represents a new low." Kane then declares that he will finish Leland's review for him and walks out of the office.

Block Three

Shot fifteen is an extreme close-up of the letters "W-E-A-K" being typed on a piece of paper. The typewriter keys smack the paper loudly. Shots sixteen and seventeen return to Leland's office. As Kane is heard typing offscreen, Leland finally wakes from his stupor and asks for his review. Bernstein informs him that Kane is finishing it, "just the way you started it."

At the beginning of shot eighteen, Kane is seen in the outer part of the city room, typing at a desk. His head and torso fill the left hand side of the frame. Leland then approaches, stopping a few feet behind Kane. In the far back, between the two men, the silhouette of Bernstein appears in the doorway of Leland's office. All three men are in focus. Light falls on Kane, especially the white of his tuxedo shirt, and on Leland.

Without looking up from the typewriter, Kane senses Leland's presence and greets him. Leland responds, talking to Kane's back:

> LELAND
> Hello, Charlie—I didn't know we were speaking.

> KANE
> Sure, we're speaking, Jedediah—
> You're fired.

> He swings [typewriter] carriage back, types. Leland is staring at him.[7]

The final shot begins with a close-up of Leland, reacting to being fired. He says nothing and slowly turns and walks out of the same glass doors that Kane came in through at the start of the scene.

Whose scene is it? Although part of Leland's recollections, the scene belongs to Kane.

What is the objective of the sequence? The objective of the city room sequence is to reunite Kane and Leland and then to close the door permanently on their friendship.

Acting

As directed by Welles, precise but understated performances are key to the sequence's success. Throughout the sequence, the movement of the actors is especially expressive. Kane starts off in the shadows of the room, but the moment he steps forward into the light, Welles puts him into center frame. Except for Leland, the other actors appear small compared to Kane. Kane, dressed in a top hat and fur coat, walks like a man in charge, stomping into Leland's office and throwing open the door.

In contrast, Leland's movements are weak and hesitant. His walk to Kane at the typewriter is drawn out and apprehensive. Leland's slow exit through the glass doors brings the sequence full circle. Leland leaves as an outsider, just as Kane entered as an outsider.

Welles, as Kane, delivers his lines with a bemused calm that betrays the fury he is feeling inside. His opponent in the scene, Leland, goes through a range of emotions in short order. Just after waking in his office, Leland has a moment of happy anticipation when he hears that Kane, an old friend he has not seen for some time, is in the next room. "Charlie?" he says with a smile. Pleasure fades as soon as Bernstein tells him that Kane is finishing his review. For a second, Leland is disappointed but resigned. When Bernstein informs him that Kane is writing a bad review, however, Leland becomes confused. Finally, when fired, he is stunned.

COMPOSITION–ANGLE, SIZE, AND POSITION

In addition to acting, Welles uses camera angles and positioning within the frame to define relationships between characters and bring out emotions.

Though they are old friends, Bernstein is subservient to Kane, his employer. In Leland's office, Kane is viewed from a low angle from behind Bernstein, looking up at the domineering Kane. Leland's collapsed body always appears between them, and Bernstein hovers over it protectively. Welles visually reinforces Leland's role as spoiler, the man who "comes between" Kane and Bernstein.

In the next block, Welles turns the tables on Leland. As he is simultaneously writing his scathing review and firing Leland, Kane keeps his back to Leland. Though he has not seen Leland for some time, Kane refuses to look him in the eye. Already he has dismissed Leland in his mind and is punishing him with his body language. Leland is left behind, literally and figuratively.

Orson Welles and cameraman Gregg Toland prepare for a low-angle shot during the filming of Citizen Kane.

Composition—Lenses

In the deep depth of field shot in block one both the subjects in the foreground—Bernstein and the others—and the subjects in the background—Kane and Leland's office—stay in sharp focus throughout the shot. The entire frame, including the corners, is packed with visual information. The ceiling of the cavernous outer room fills the top of the frame and reporters and desks are placed all through the large set.

By keeping all of the characters in the same shot, equally focused, Welles greatly increases the tension of the moment. The audience can observe Bernstein's anxiety increase as Kane gets closer and closer to Leland's office.

The long shot of Kane typing at the end of the sequence appears to be deep focus but was actually achieved in post-production as a visual effect. It nevertheless functions in much the same way as the block one deep-focus shot. Welles connects all three characters—Bernstein, Leland, and Kane—in a visual triangle that echoes the tense emotional triangle they are enacting.

Composition—Lighting

Lighting in the sequence, particularly in the first and third blocks, is typical of lighting elsewhere in the picture. Welles contrasts the dark areas with blindingly bright light. The light in the hallway outside the city room door and the white of the men's tuxedo shirts pop out at the viewer.

Throughout the sequence, Welles separates people with shadows, most notably in the first shot and final shots. Kane, who has never visited the city room before, waits in the shadows upon first arriving, then steps into the light like a king. In the last shot, Kane and Leland occupy separate pools of light, divided by a telling island of darkness.

Editing

Although the city room sequence is one shot shorter than the Xanadu opening, it runs over two minutes longer. With a few exceptions, shots in the opening sequence are about the same length. In the later scene, however, they vary in length. Blocks one and three consist of long takes, but shots in the middle block are mostly short.

Like deep-focus photography, longer takes in the first and third blocks enhance the suspense of the scene. They keep the audience in the moment, a visual equivalent of holding one's breath.

The goal of block two, however, is to reveal what Leland has been writing and to show Kane's reaction to it. By breaking the scene up into a series of over-the-shoulder and reaction shots, Welles increases the film's tempo. The viewer feels the tension and senses the anger rising in Kane. As Kane releases his anger in the final segment, the tempo slows and fades.

Sound

Unlike the opening sequence, no music is heard in the city room sequence. Instead Welles uses sounds—in particular the drumlike sounds of the typewriter—to underline the characters' feelings. Kane is obviously furious with Leland for criticizing his wife but acts outwardly cool and in control. Only the pounding, smacking sounds of the typewriter reveal what Kane is really feeling.

Putting It All Together:
The Sixth Sense

Released in August 1999, *The Sixth Sense* was a box-office phenomenon. Twenty-nine-year-old writer/director M. Night Shyamalan was a relative Hollywood newcomer and although Bruce Willis was a major star, no other cast member was well known. Despite modest box office expectations, the film went on to become one of the highest grossing movies of all time. It also received six major Academy Award nominations, including Best Director and Best Picture.

Key to the film's success was its surprise ending. Not revealing the plot twist became part of the movie's mystique. Even today viewers are reluctant to discuss the film's ending. Since *The Sixth Sense*, surprise endings have become a trademark of Shyamalan's work.

Shyamalan cites Alfred Hitchcock and Steven Spielberg as his primary artistic influences. Like Hitchcock, Shyamalan is attracted to tightly constructed suspense stories. He likes to pull the audience into the world of his movies and play with their expectations. Also like Hitchcock, Shyamalan does storyboards for every scene and prepares thoroughly before shooting. And he always appears in his films, another Hitchcock trait.

Shyamalan's movies resemble Spielberg's in theme and tone. Like Spielberg, Shyamalan is fascinated by the theme of family and how children perceive the world. In tone, Shyamalan's movies have great warmth, like many of Spielberg's films. Much of that warmth comes out of the actors' performances. Shyamalan prefers to work with accomplished actors, sometimes casting against type. When he was cast in *The Sixth Sense*, for example, Bruce Willis was known primarily as an action star.

THE STORY

One night, renowned Philadelphia child psychiatrist Dr. Malcolm Crowe (Bruce Willis) is confronted in his home by a former patient who shoots Malcolm and then kills himself. Months later, a seemingly recovered Malcolm meets Cole Sear (Haley Joel Osment). Cole, whose parents have recently divorced, is suffering from acute anxiety. At the same time, Malcolm has apparently become estranged from his own wife, Anna (Olivia Williams).

Eventually Cole reveals to Malcolm that he keeps seeing ghosts—all of whom died violent deaths. Malcolm suggests that these ghosts may be trying to tell Cole something. Cole then speaks to the ghost of a girl named Kyra Collins (Mischa Barton) and helps save Kyra's little sister.

Malcolm, meanwhile, has an unexpected revelation. While standing over the sleeping Anna, he sees himself bleeding and realizes that he is himself a

Bruce Willis and Haley Joel Osment in a scene from M. Night Shyamalan's The Sixth Sense *(1999).*

ghost. With this realization, Malcolm departs, freeing Anna to live and love again.

THE RULES

In interviews about *The Sixth Sense*, Shyamalan revealed that he and his collaborators—cinematographer Tak Fujimoto, production designer Larry Fulton, and costume designer Joanna Johnston—enacted "rules" to keep the supernatural elements of the story consistent.

According to the rules, the presence of red in a scene indicated that the living world had been tainted by the "other world." Ghostly encounters were always signaled by red objects, usually in a character's clothes but also in the surrounding décor. Sudden cold and frosty breath announced the arrival of angry ghosts. Because Malcolm is never angry around Cole, Cole does not feel cold, as he does with the other ghosts.

Throughout the film, Malcolm wears the same outfit he was wearing the night of his death, from winter coat to dress shirt and tie. Because of its layers and neutral style, first-time audiences remain unaware that his clothes never change during the movie. Shyamalan was also careful to stage Malcolm's movements so that other actors and objects would not intersect with him and expose his "ghostliness."

SHOT-BY-SHOT ANALYSIS

The Sequence—Guilty!

One of the most elaborate and dramatic sequences in *The Sixth Sense* occurs near the end of the picture, when Cole and Malcolm go to Kyra Collins' house. In the sequence are many of the storytelling techniques and rules that Shyamalan uses throughout the movie.

In the two scenes immediately preceding the sequence, the ghost Kyra appears in Cole's bedroom. She vomits and then declares that she is feeling better. At first Cole panics, then gets his courage up and asks if there is something she wants to tell him. Before the audience hears her answer, the film jumps ahead to show Cole and Malcolm riding a city bus to Kyra's house.

Block One

The thirty-shot sequence runs eight minutes and starts with a crane shot showing Cole and Malcolm arriving for Kyra's funeral reception. It is a sunny Fall day on an upscale suburban street. Black-clad mourners are exiting cars and making their way to the Collins house. Cole and Malcolm walk into the frame from the right and blend in with the group.

The camera then cranes down and around to a full shot, focusing on a distraught woman and her two male companions, standing frame right. As one of the men leaves to get water for the woman, the camera moves with him, picking up Cole and

93

Malcolm as they pass a swing set on Kyra's front lawn.

The camera continues to track left, and Cole informs Malcolm that the little girl on the swing is Kyra's sister (Samantha Fitzpatrick). The second shot is a Steadicam shot, taken inside Kyra's living room, where the reception is in full swing. The camera weaves among the mourners, picking up their whispered comments about Kyra. One mourner states that Kyra had been sick for two years; another notes that Kyra's sister has also fallen ill.

The camera finally returns to Cole and Malcolm as they head up a staircase. The shot ends with the camera zeroing in on a close-up of a Collins family portrait hanging on the staircase wall.

Shot three is a medium, low-angle shot featuring Cole and Malcolm in the upstairs hallway. Cole is in the foreground, staring ahead apprehensively; Malcolm stands behind him.

Shot four consists of a close-up of a doorknob, with Cole's image clearly reflected in the metal. As he reaches for the knob, Cole tells Malcolm not to go home. Malcolm agrees.

Block Two

Shot five opens on darkness. The frame slowly fills with hallway light as Cole opens the door. The music grows increasingly ominous.

The next two medium close-ups focus on objects in the room—first a shelf with videotapes, then a shelf with dolls. Cole reaches into the left side of the frame and picks up a clown finger puppet.

Shot eight is a long shot of Cole standing near a wall to the left of a neatly made hospital-style bed. The view of Cole is obstructed by several marionettes hanging on strings in the foreground. The puppets begin to sway a little, attracting Cole's attention. As the music swells, Cole walks forward, intently watching the puppets. Suddenly, with a musical thud, an arm thrusts out from under the bed toward Cole's leg. Cole screams and falls back.

Shot nine finds Cole on the floor, pressed against the wall, panting in terror. The camera swish-pans clockwise to reveal the ghost Kyra crouched under the bed. Without a word Kyra shoves a red-striped wooden box toward Cole. The camera then swish-pans counter-clockwise back to Cole and dollies into a close-up of his panicked face.

Block Three

Shot ten is another long Steadicam shot taken in the living room. The camera observes Cole carrying the red-striped box, regarding the guests as though searching for a particular person. He passes by Kyra's mother, a blonde woman in a bright red dress who is being consoled by another mourner. Finally, Cole spots a man seated in the adjoining den. The camera tracks around and behind the man, as Cole approaches him.

Cole stops in front of the man and confirms that he is Mr. Collins, Kyra's father (Greg Wood). Malcolm steps into the background of the shot, out of focus but visible. He watches as Cole hands Mr. Collins the box. "She wanted to tell you something," Cole says. Cole then walks back to Malcolm, and they both exit left.

Shot eleven is a close-up on the box, with the red stripe dominating the frame. Mr. Collins opens the lid to reveal a video tape.

Haley Joel Osment and Toni Collette in a key scene from **The Sixth Sense.**

Block Four

Shots twelve through twenty-four show the contents of the tape and Mr. Collins' reaction to it. As the tape begins to play on the den television set, the music score stops. The video images are realistically fuzzy and at a fixed angle. The first few moments of the tape, recorded by Kyra in her bedroom, are seemingly innocent. On a miniature puppet stage, Kyra plays with the marionettes seen in shot eight. She appears happy and her childish joking brings a small smile to Mr. Collins' teary face.

Kyra reacts to an offscreen noise and quickly puts away the stage and hops into her bed. Mrs. Collins (Angelica Torn) enters the frame carrying a tray with food. She sets the tray down in front of the camera, unaware that it is still on and filming her actions.

The camera records Mrs. Collins, her back to Kyra, retrieving and then pouring a strange chemical into a bowl of soup on the tray. At that point, the camera moves closer on the TV set and closer on Mr. Collins. With each reaction shot, his facial expression changes, from curiosity to pleasure to confusion to shock.

In shot twenty-two, the video shows Mrs. Collins sliding the tray onto Kyra's lap. She tells Kyra that she cannot play outside after lunch because she always gets "sick in the afternoon." With motherly concern, Mrs. Collins then tells Kyra not to complain about the soup tasting "funny."

In shot twenty-three, the camera dollies into a close-up of Mr. Collins, his eyes filling with tears as his mind grasps what he has just seen. A group of guests has gathered behind him and are watching the video with him.

Shot twenty-four returns to the video tape, but from a closer angle. In this non-realistic, subjective shot, Kyra eats her mother's poisoned soup.

Block Five

The next medium shot zeroes in on Mrs. Collins, the blonde woman in red. Her back is to the camera, but when the room suddenly goes quiet, she turns, perplexed, to face her husband.

Shot twenty-six begins as a medium shot of Mr. Collins, standing just inside the den. Surrounding him are guests, their grim, shocked expressions revealing all. In an uneven, jerky motion, the camera pushes in to a close-up of the crying Mr. Collins.

Shot twenty-seven returns to Mrs. Collins. A hand-held camera again moves in on her heavily made up face.

Block Six

Shot twenty-eight shifts to another part of the house. The swing set in the front yard is seen through the blinds of a window. Outside, Cole is sitting on a swing next to Kyra's sister. Malcolm stands next to the set, somewhat detached.

The next shot is an over-the-shoulder shot from behind Cole. He hands Kyra's sister the finger puppet, noting that Kyra had said that her sister liked it. The girl then asks Cole if Kyra is coming back.

The final shot of the sequence is a high-angle shot looking down on Malcolm, who is facing left. Offscreen, Cole answers the girl's question, "Not anymore." Touched by the exchange, Malcolm turns away, and the screen fades to black.

How Does It Work?

The marvel of *The Sixth Sense* is that it succeeds as both a genre horror movie and as a serious drama. In a video interview, Shyamalan described his job on the project: "When you make a film there are all different steps. You can come up with an idea and you write the screenplay. And then you hire the actors and then you go to the set and you shoot the movie. And then you edit the movie and you put sound to it and you put music to it. You check the color. And then it goes out to the theaters."[1]

Shyamalan makes the process sound simple and straightforward, but in order to create both a ghost story and a story of redemption, great thought had to be put into every moment of the picture. The Kyra sequence exemplifies this care.

Whose scene is it? Although Malcolm is the protagonist of the film, the Kyra sequence belongs to Cole. Malcolm appears as emotional support for Cole, and witnessing Cole's transformation is necessary for Malcolm's own resolution as a character. Cole's actions, however, are the focus of the sequence, even when he is not onscreen.

What is the goal of the sequence? The goal is to show Cole taking control of his special ability, his sixth sense, and overcoming his fears. The sequence is the turning point of the story. Once Cole has faced his fears and helped Kyra, the story is ready to conclude.

The Moving Camera

As a director Shyamalan favors traveling shots and long takes. *The Sixth Sense* is full of them. In fact, another key scene in the movie—where Malcolm finds Anna commemorating their anniversary in a restaurant—is comprised of a single traveling shot. The Kyra sequence has three long traveling shots, all motivated by Cole.

At their most basic, the first two traveling shots of block one are establishing shots. Very efficiently, the locale is shown, inside and out. Kyra's well-to-do neighborhood is contrasted with Cole's working-class home. The audience gets a sense of geography, especially the location of the swing set, which comes into play at the end of the sequence.

The traveling shots also have a symbolic function. Despite Malcolm's presence in the sequence, Cole is a small boy negotiating his way in an adult world. The traveling camera reminds the audience of the journey he is on. He is moving forward, along with the camera. This fact is particu-

100

larly noticeable in the third traveling shot, when Cole searches the living room for Mr. Collins. The camera is in effect searching with him.

The traveling shots also help create a feeling of community. As the camera shows, Kyra is being mourned not just by her immediate family, but by many others as well. Shyamalan emphasizes this point when, in the opening crane shot, he moves away from Cole and Malcolm to focus on a grieving woman. In the second traveling shot, Shyamalan continues the feeling by focusing on comments of the mourners. The comments not only convey important plot information, they also connect the guests to Kyra.

Many other shots in the sequence feature symbolic camera movement. Some are subtle dollies in on characters' faces, others are jarring, frenzied pans and jerky hand-held moves. All of these movements help draw the audience into the emotional world of the film. The swish pans in the bedroom scene convey Cole's terror, while the dollied close-ups of Mr. Collins underline his growing anxiety about Kyra's death. The back-to-back hand-held shots mirror the devastating blow to the family unit that the video tape produces.

Composition

As many critics have observed, Shyamalan loves "reflective" shots—shots in which the reflected image of a character is seen. Shyamalan reflects images in mirrors, glasses, window panes, shiny

Directing the actions of Bruce Willis in **The Sixth Sense** *required a very subtle hand in order to preserve the film's suspense.*

metals, and any other surface that produces a mirror effect. In the opening sequence of the movie, for example, Shyamalan includes several shots of Malcolm and Anna reflected in the glass of a framed award that Malcolm has just received.

In the Kyra sequence Cole's upper body and the side of Malcolm's body, are shown reflected in the doorknob of Kyra's bedroom door. Visually, the image is unexpected and disorienting. It reinforces the feeling of dread evident on Cole's face. Symbolically, it is another way to represent Cole's sixth sense. Wherever Cole goes, another world is always looking back at him.

Shyamalan includes a second reflective surface in the wooden box containing the video tape. The inside of the box lid is mirrored, and when Mr. Collins opens it, a reflection of the tape appears. Along with the view of the actual tape, which is solid and real, is a mirrored view. The reflected image represents Cole's ghost world, a message from the "other side."

Point of View

Shyamalan's staging allows the viewer to experience the sequence through different points of view. When Cole first enters Kyra's bedroom in block two, for example, the shots are from his point of view—the audience sees the video tapes and the finger puppets as Cole sees them. In the next shot, however, Cole is seen from a distance, partially obscured by Kyra's marionettes.

Suddenly, the audience senses Cole is being watched. (To heighten the element of surprise, Shyamalan also uses this shot to distract the audience's attention away from the bed where Kyra's ghost is hiding.) The swish-pan between Cole and Kyra further reinforces the dual point of view. He stares at her, then she stares at him.

In blocks four and five, the point of view shifts to Mr. Collins. By giving him the tape, Cole is in essence handing Kyra over to him. The audience watches the tape, Kyra's from-the-grave accusation, from his point of view.

None of the sequence is seen through Malcolm's point of view. Instead Shyamalan stages the sequence so that Cole can act as Malcolm's guide. When they first arrive at the house, Cole points out Kyra's sister on the swing. "That's her sister," he says. Cole then leads Malcolm upstairs. Malcolm stands behind him in the hallway, and later, when Cole hands the box to Mr. Collins, Malcolm shows up in the background of the shot, watching Cole. The audience also watches Malcolm as he watches Cole talking to Kyra's sister.

Shyamalan ends the sequence squarely on Malcolm. The high-angle shot—looking down on Malcolm from above—which accompanies Cole's statement that Kyra is not coming back, suggests Kyra's ghostly point of view. Significantly Malcolm, the unknowing ghost, is the focus of her gaze.

Color

In keeping with the rules of the movie's narrative, Shyamalan uses the color red to announce the presence of ghosts in the sequence. The red stripe on the wooden box is one instance of "ghost" red. Most notable, however, is the red dress that Mrs. Collins wears. She is the only mourner not dressed in dark colors. The red of her dress (and lipstick) make her stand out visually, and it signals the presence of ghosts.

The intensity of the red dress also makes the viewer think of blood and danger. Through the color red, Shyamalan reveals to the audience that Mrs. Collins not only has been infected by the other world, she also has her daughter's blood on her. She is not a grieving mother, but a dangerous killer.

Sound and Music

Sound and music are vital to the drama of *The Sixth Sense.* Early on in the production process, Shyamalan began thinking about how to use music and sound to represent the reality of the "sixth sense." Shyamalan states in the video interview that he asked composer John Newton Howard to imagine Cole's sixth sense as an "invisible animal in the room that you hear crawling and moving around you. You're not sure where it is but you feel threatened by it."[2]

In the same video interview, Howard said about his conversations with Shyamalan: "He would talk about the sixth sense almost as a living entity that is . . . morphing throughout, from room to room in the house and appearing in this sort of liquid way."[3]

For the sound design, Shyamalan wanted "to create a moving ambiance in the movie so that in empty rooms you feel that there's a presence. It's not a literal thing, but through the course of the movie you feel very uneasy."[4] To achieve that unease, Shyamalan and sound designer/editor Michael Kirchberger added breaths to the background of the soundtrack. "Human breaths—men, women, children, everyone. Hundreds of breaths are in the movie . . . lizard breath, bear breath, human breath."[5] Although not easy to distinguish on the soundtrack, these breaths are present in the Kyra sequence.

Along with background breathing sounds, Shyamalan also directed the actors to sigh and pant during many of the scenes. In the Kyra sequence, Cole pants heavily when he encounters Kyra in the bedroom. Like the beating of a heart, the sound of breathing represents life. Cole is alive, Kyra is not.

In the Kyra sequence, Howard's score and Kirchberger's sounds echo the conflict of the drama. The music begins quietly and gently. At the end of block one when Cole reaches for the doorknob, the score becomes instantly sinister. As Cole looks around Kyra's room, the little bells on Kyra's puppets ring as the puppets begin to sway. The music grows ominous, then explodes the moment Kyra's arm thrusts out from under the bed.

Cole's fear subsides and so does the music. While he carries the wooden box to Mr. Collins, the bell sound—Kyra's sound—is repeated in the music. The music cuts out during the first part of the video, but resumes dramatically the very moment that Mr. Collins realizes what his wife has done. The tinkling bells return in the final block, when Cole hands Kyra's sister the finger puppet.

A CAREER IN DIRECTING

People come to film directing from a variety of backgrounds, talents, and personalities. Since good directing requires a little bit of knowledge about a lot of disciplines, no particular type of education or skill set is required. Some directors begin as stage directors or actors, some as writers, others as visual artists or even musicians. One trait present in all directors, however, is the ability and willingness to make decisions, big and small, artistic as well as practical.

ON BECOMING A FILMMAKER

Veteran filmmakers love to share stories about their careers. Below are thoughts and advice from a few directors.

Mike Figgis (*Leaving Las Vegas*, *Coma*) recalls his youth in London, where he first became interested in filmmaking: "I saw a short there called *Incident at Owl Creek*, which really influenced me. At the same time, I was totally into music. I joined an avant garde free jazz group and started working with a theater company. I think that set-up the idea that you don't separate the arts; that painting and music and cinema are very closely related."[1]

Ang Lee (*Crouching Tiger, Hidden Dragon, Brokeback Mountain*), who began his professional career as a stage actor, describes his journey to filmmaking this way: "It was at high school that my mind started drifting. I was a very shy, introverted, spaced-out kid. . . . When my father asked me before I got into high school what I wanted to do in the future, I said I wanted to be a film director and everybody just laughed. Nobody took me seriously. . . . So I think from very early on I dreamt about making fantasies on the screen."[2]

John Singleton (*Boyz in the Hood, Four Brothers*), who attended the University of Southern California's film writing program and made his first feature when he was only twenty-three, offers this perspective: "I grew up in South Central Los Angeles, and went to Hollywood to hang out when I was a kid and a teenager, and I developed a love for the power of film. That's what drew me to film school, cinema was my rite of passage. . . . When I was nine years old I went to see *Star Wars*, like ten times, and

Director Ang Lee on the red carpet at the 78th Annual Academy Awards in 2006.

I started breaking down how they made the shots, and studying how to make a film. And I started making animated films on the sides of notebooks, because the power of the moving image was very intriguing to me. . . . I'm influenced by not only Kurosawa, but also Marvin Gaye and Tupac. So I'm coming at it a whole other way."[3]

Indian-born **Mira Nair** (*Monsoon Wedding*, *Vanity Fair*), who went from acting to making documentaries before becoming a feature director, says: "I wasn't one of those people who grew up knowing I was a filmmaker or making movies in my backyard or anything of the sort. I grew up in a small town, with one cinema, that was remote even in Indian terms. The only thing I remember which has carried into making movies is that I loved getting involved with people's lives."[4]

Sam Raimi (*Spider Man*) adds: "I do think there's a new crop of American filmmakers coming. And they're in high school right now. They're in Mrs. Dawson's English class! They've got new tools, they've got computers and the video cameras, which are the equivalent of our super-8mm training ground. It's even better because they can shoot for free. We had to gather up like four bucks, five bucks to buy a roll of film, another three bucks to process it, and that was a very limiting [thing]. In high school you gotta rake leaves for three hours to shoot a roll of

Director John Singleton on the set of the film, 2 Fast 2 Furious *(2003)*.

film! So these new filmmakers have these advanced editing tools with the incredible manipulation of imagery available on a standard computer."[5]

VIDEO ON THE WEB

The World Wide Web has proven to be an excellent outlet for filmmakers who are just starting out. Sites such as YouTube, Google video, Yahoo! video, and iFilm allow their users to put their original videos on display for the whole world to see. These and other websites have spawned the phenomenon of "viral video"—which is what happens when a video file is emailed/ shared with friends, who in turn forward the video to their other friends, who forward it to still other friends, and so on. This is a quick and easy way to reach the public with your film, but getting your work noticed could be difficult. YouTube, for example, had 9 million unique visitors to its site in February 2006, and was showing more than 40 million videos a day at that time.[6]

CONTINUING EDUCATION

According to a 2005 *New York Times* article, over 600 colleges and universities in the United States offer programs in film studies or related subjects. Many of those offer degrees in film production. High school graduates can also attend one-year (non-degree) film schools.

Schools with filmmaking programs are located not only in California, but across the United States

Sam Raimi gives directions to actors Tobey Maguire and Kirsten Dunst on the set of Spider-Man 2 *(2004).*

and Canada. Below is a partial list of four-year colleges that offer degrees in film-production:

- Auburn University: Auburn, Alabama
- Brigham Young University: Provo, Utah
- Chapman University: Orange, California
- Colorado Film School: Denver, Colorado (AGS, AAS and BFA degrees)
- Drexel University: Philadelphia, Pennsylvania
- Depaul University: Chicago, Illinois (Digital Cinema)

113

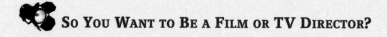

- Florida State University Film School: Tallahassee, Florida
- Loyola Marymount University: Los Angeles, California
- Middlebury College: Middlebury, Vermont
- New York University, Tisch School of the Arts: New York City, New York
- North Carolina School of the Arts: Winston-Salem, North Carolina
- Nova Scotia College of Art and Design: Halifax, Nova Scotia, Canada
- Pennsylvania State: University Park, Pennsylvania
- Regent University: Virginia Beach, Virginia
- Ryerson University: Toronto, Ontario, Canada
- San Diego State University: San Diego, California
- San Francisco State University: San Francisco, California
- School of Visual Arts: New York, New York
- SUNY College at Purchase: Purchase, New York
- University of California, Berkeley: Berkeley, California
- University of California, Los Angeles (UCLA): Los Angeles, California
- University of Central Florida School of Film & Digital Media: Orlando, Florida
- University of Kansas: Lawrence, Kansas
- University of Michigan: Ann Arbor, Michigan
- University of North Texas: Denton, Texas
- University of Oklahoma: Norman, Oklahoma
- University of Southern California: Los Angeles, California
- University of Texas: Austin, Texas

- University of Wisconsin: Milwaukee, Wisconsin

The following community colleges offer two-year degrees in film production:

- Colorado Film School: Denver, Colorado (AGS, AAS and BFA degrees)
- Los Angeles Community College: Los Angeles, California
- Minneapolis Community and Technical College: Minneapolis, Minnesota
- Scottsdale Community College: Scottsdale, Arizona

In addition, the New York Film Academy, which has branches in New York City, Los Angeles, and London, has a one-year diploma program in filmmaking. The Academy also offers a special summer program for high school students.

FILM CONTESTS— YOU CAN DO IT TOO!

Today's digital and computer technology has revolutionized moviemaking. As filmmaking tools become cheaper to buy and simpler to use, more and more young people are experimenting with moviemaking. In response to the growing number of teen "Spielbergs," various organizations and schools have begun sponsoring young filmmaker contests.

The following is a partial list of contests geared specifically toward the teen filmmaker.

115

Director Salaries

Starting Salary	Experienced Salary	Star Salary
As low as $10,000	Up to $200,000–300,000	Millions (?)

Unless they are working regularly on a TV series, directors make a highly unpredictable living—particularly when they are just starting out. (And even on a TV series, income is lost when a show goes on hiatus or if it is suddenly cancelled.) Experienced Directors make more per project, but again it is by contract and the amount varies widely. Weekly union salaries can vary between $10,000 (a theatrical short or documentary) up to $92,000 a week for a prime-time, big-budget, two-hour TV program. But obviously directors do not work every week, and many are not getting paid union wages. (Some use their own money to finance their films and end up with credit card debt instead of a salary!)

Hot Shots High School Film and Ad Festival. Open to students under nineteen. Various categories.
    Web site: http://www.hsfilmfest.com/

Movie Gallery Student Video Competition/High School Videomaker Category. Various categories.
    Web site: http://www.auburn.edu/student_info/film/contest.htm

National Neighborhood Day Short Film Contest/Youth Category. Open to students 18 and under.
    Web site: http://www.neighborhoodday.org/film.asp

CHAPTER NOTES

CHAPTER 1. ELEMENTS OF DIRECTING: FROM THE SCRIPT TO THE SHOT

1. Robert J. Emery, *The Directors: Take Four* (New York: Allworth Press, 2003), p. 108.

2. Sidney Lumet, *Making Movies* (New York: Alfred A. Knopf, 1995), p. 10.

3. Robert J. Emery, *The Directors: Take Three* (New York: Allworth Press, 2003), p. 65.

4. Louis D. Giannetti, *Understanding Movies,* 2nd ed. (Englewood Cliffs, N.J.: Prentice-Hall, 1976), p. 49.

5. Lumet, p. 88.

6. Iain Bruce, "The Village: Q and A with M. Night Shyamalan," December 8, 2004, <http://talkfilm.co.uk/articles/244/> (March 8, 2006).

7. Lumet, p. 103.

8. Mark Woods, "Lens Personalities," n.d., <http://www.cameraguild.com/technology/lens.htm> (March 8, 2006).

9. Peter Brunette, ed., *Martin Scorsese: Interviews* (Jackson, Miss.: University Press of Mississippi, 1999), p. 214.

10. Emery, *The Directors: Take Three*, pp. 215–16.

11. Lumet, p. 81.

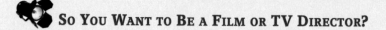

Chapter 2. Elements of Directing: Staging the Scene

1. Emery, *The Directors: Take Three*, p. 200.
2. Emery, *The Directors: Take Four*, p. 217.
3. Personal interview with Lee Shallat Chemel, May 16, 2005.
4. Ibid.
5. Ibid.
6. Ibid.

Chapter 3. Elements of Directing: Post-Production

1. Lumet, p. 161.
2. Ibid.
3. Michael Jarrett, "Sound Doctrine: An Interview with Walter Murch," n.d., <http://www2.yk.psu.edu/~jmj3/murchfq.htm> (March 8, 2006).
4. Ibid.
5. Lumet, p. 170.
6. Ibid., p. 173.

Chapter 4. Directing for Television

1. Shallat Chemel.
2. Ibid.

Chapter 5. Putting It All Together: Citizen Kane

1. Bosley Crowther, *The New York Times*, May 2, 1941, p. 25.
2. Ephraim Katz, *The Film Encyclopedia* (New York: HarperCollins, 1994), p. 1443.

3. Gregg Toland, "Making *Citizen Kane,*" *American Cinematographer*, February 1941, p. 54.

4. Ibid., p. 55.

5. Ibid.

6. Giannetti, p. 191.

7. Herman J. Mankiewicz and Orson Welles, *The* Citizen Kane *Book: The Shooting Script* (New York: Limelight Editions, 1984), pp. 394–95.

CHAPTER 6. PUTTING IT ALL TOGETHER: *THE SIXTH SENSE*

1. The Sixth Sense*: Collectors Edition Series* (Buena Vista Home Entertainment and Spyglass Entertainment Group, 2000).

2. Ibid.

3. Ibid.

4. Ibid.

5. Ibid.

CHAPTER 7. A CAREER IN DIRECTING

1. Stephen Lowenstein, ed. *My First Movie* (London: Penguin Books, 2002), p. 274.

2. Ibid., pp. 361–62.

3. Cynthia Fuchs, "Interview with John Singleton," n.d. <http://www.popmatters.com/film/interviews/singleton/john.html> (March 8, 2006).

4. Lowenstein, p. 245.

5. Ray Pride, "Within That Darkness," October 20, 2004, <http://www.newcitychicago.com/chicago/3812.html> (March 8, 2006).

6. Lev Grossman, "How to Get Famous in 30 Seconds," *TIME*, April 24, 2006, p. 66.

GLOSSARY

aerial shot—A high exterior shot, usually taken from a helicopter.

aspect ratio—The ratio of the width of an image to its height.

auteur **theory**—A theory of film criticism that emphasizes the director as the major creator.

bird's-eye view—A shot in which the camera films a scene from directly overhead.

blocking—A plan for moving actors in a scene.

cinematographer—The technician responsible for photographing a scene and often for the overall look of a film. Also called director of photography.

close-up—A detailed view of a person or object. A close-up of an actor usually includes only the head.

composition—The organization or grouping of different elements in an image.

continuity—The illusion of a real or logical sequence of events across a series of film cuts.

coverage—Shots that depict all of the action of a scene.

crane shot—A shot taken from a crane, a device that resembles a large mechanical arm.

cross-cutting—The alternating of shots from two sequences, usually in different locations, to suggest the action is going on at the same time.

depth of field—The distance in front of the camera lens within which objects appear in sharp focus.

dissolve—The slow fading out of one shot and the gradual fading in of the next, with the two shots overlapping halfway.

dolly shot—A traveling shot on which the camera is mounted on a small, heavy unit, or dolly, that moves along a track. Also called tracking shot.

dubbing—The addition of sound after the visuals have been photographed.

editing—The joining or splicing together of one shot with another.

establishing shot—A shot that gives the viewer an overview of a scene setting, usually coming at the beginning of a scene.

expressionism—A style of filmmaking that distorts time and space and emphasizes basic qualities of people and objects.

exterior location—An outdoor setting where filming occurs.

eye-level shot—A shot in which the camera is placed between five to six feet from the ground.

fade-in/out—The gradual fading of an image from normal brightness to black screen (fade-out); or the gradual brightening of an image from black screen to normal brightness (fade-in).

filter—A piece of glass or plastic placed in front of the camera lens, which changes the quality of the light entering the camera.

fine cut—The final stage of editing a film.

flashback—A scene from the past that interrupts the ongoing action.

foreground—The parts of an image that appear in the front.

frame—A single image or photograph from a strip of film; or the borders encompassing the image.

full shot—A type of long shot that includes the actor's body in full, with the head near the top of the frame and the feet near the bottom.

high key—Lighting that emphasizes bright, even illumination, with few shadows.

low key—Lighting that emphasizes soft shadows and pools of light.

master shot—A single continuous shot that contains the action of an entire scene.

mise-en-scène—The arrangement of objects and their movement within a shot.

montage—Film editing, particularly editing in which images are connected thematically.

music scoring—Musical composition written for a particular film.

narrative block—A group of actions within a scene that are unified by a common dramatic objective.

normal lens—A camera lens that approximates human vision.

oblique angle—A shot filmed by a tilted camera, which makes the subjects appear tilted within the frame.

outtake—A take that is removed from the shot footage.

pan—Revolving horizontal movement of the camera from left to right, or vice-versa.

parallel action—Two or more actions that take place at the same time in different spaces.

point-of-view shot (POV)—A shot approximating the view of a specific character.

post-production—The phase of film production that occurs after principal photography has been completed.

principal photography—The main photography of a film and the period during which it takes place.

production designer—Person responsible for the look and feel of a film's setting and costumes.

protagonist—The main character of a narrative; the character who engages the reader's interest and sympathy.

rack focus—To shift focus from one subject to another in a shot, usually from foreground to background.

retakes—Shots that are filmed more than once, often after principal photography.

reverse-angle shot—A shot in which the camera is placed opposite to its previous position.

rough cut—The crudely edited total footage of a film.

scene—A unit of film composed of a number of shots connected by a common setting.

shot—Those images that are filmed continuously from the time the camera starts to the time it stops.

soundtrack—The audio portion of a film.

stage directions—A scriptwriter's written instructions about how the actors and, in some cases, the camera, are to move and behave. Also known as the descriptive text.

Steadicam—A device that enables the cameraman to hold the camera while achieving the same balance and steadiness as a mounted or tracking camera.

storyboard—A sketch or series of sketches that depicts how part or all of a scene is to be staged.

swish-pan—A rapid horizontal movement of the camera around its axis, which causes the image to blur.

synchronized sound—Image and sound are recorded at the same time.

take—One version of a planned shot, as recorded during production.

thematic editing—Editing in which images are cut together based on their dramatic meaning.

tilt—A shot in which the camera pivots vertically, up and down.

tracking shot—Usually, a traveling shot for which tracks are laid down for the camera to roll on. Also known as a dolly shot.

traveling shot—A shot in which the camera moves on a vehicle while filming.

two-shot—A medium shot featuring two actors.

FURTHER READING

Books

Donald, Ralph and Spann, Thomas. *Fundamentals of Television Production*. Ames, IA: Iowa State University Press, 2000.

Giannetti, Louis D. *Understanding Movies*, 10th ed. Upper Saddle River, NJ: Pearson/Prentice Hall, 2005.

Lowenstein, Stephen, ed. *My First Movie: Twenty Celebrated Directors Talk About Their First Film*. New York: Penguin Books, 2002.

Proferes, Nicholas. *Film Directing Fundamentals*. Boston: Focal Press, 2005.

Internet Addresses

The Filmmaking Portal
http://www.filmmaking.com/

Resources and Community for Independent Filmmakers
http://www.filmmaking.net/

American Film Institute
http://www.afi.com/

INDEX